EPISTLE TO THE SKEPTICS

Other Books by David Wesley Soper

MEN WHO SHAPE BELIEF

HIGHWAYS TO FAITH

MAJOR VOICES IN AMERICAN THEOLOGY

ROOM FOR IMPROVEMENT

THESE FOUND THE WAY

Epistle to the Skeptics

By DAVID WESLEY SOPER

ASSOCIATION PRESS • NEW YORK

To Bill, Rae, Stephen Michael,
Ann Mary, and Lynn Jean

FOREWORD

THE FOLLOWING pages attempt to take the skeptic
seriously, to talk not *at* him, but *with* him—to look out
upon the world as he looks out upon it, to regard him not
as an enemy, an outcast, a madman, but a fellow member
of the human race, a fellow participant in the enterprise
of logic and life, a fellow seeker after truth and sanity,
responding to the common summons to the better and the
more.

The false frequently holds the attention of us all; often
enough it diverts us all from the course. All the more
reason that, together, we seek the true—the nature, the
demand, and the gift of reality. No man is beyond the
pale; no man is outside the school of existence; neither
atheist nor apostle is outside the sustaining, thrusting,
correcting, guiding, renewing, and rewarding operation of
the real, the true, and the sane.

The forward movement of the whole family of mankind
out of the shadows into the light is worth our common
enterprise of discovery—worth even the risks, the errors
we are bound to make. The Dark Ages are still with us;
they may last longer than we think. The Dawn is ahead

of us, yet streaks of light shine toward us from the future. There is work enough for us all; the real, the true, and the sane are not against us; they are our strength, our cleansing, and our hope. Unreality, untruth, and insanity are our only enemies. We struggle to see what we can; we pay our penny and make our choice—for creativity or cowardice; and this is our measure as men.

Let it be clearly understood that this book is a personal letter, an attempt at honest, simple, "direct communication"—from mind to mind. For this reason documentation, quotation, the piling of authority upon authority, have been ascetically eliminated or kept to a minimum. The skeptic, like any hard-working human, whether scholar or layman, upon occasion wants to get to the point, desires no scribal sand thrown in his eyes, demands that the writer addressing him shall not only "mean what he says," but "say what he means." Whatever our success or failure, we have tried to meet this demand, to avoid the "indirect communication" of "heavy" writing—elsewhere wholly legitimate and necessary, as in a monograph of, by, and for "professionals."

Each chapter begins with a section of my own experience as a pilgrim—struggling with the two demands of skepticism and faith (of honest questioning and necessary action). No two experiences are exactly identical, yet all men live within one reality, however diversely interpreted. Some abstract argument is essential to my purpose; for this reason specially I have begun each chapter with concrete material, readily available to anyone. The reader will remember identical or divergent phases of his own pilgrimage.

As independent series, these chapters with added technical material were presented in six lectures, on the Oxford University Faculty of Theology, during Trinity term, 1955—at both Mansfield College (Congregational) and Manchester College (Unitarian). My thanks to Principal

Sydney Spencer of Manchester and Principal John Marsh of Mansfield for these opportunities, for their friendship and co-operation, and to the members of both Senior and Junior Common Rooms for their fellowship in question and comment.

DAVID WESLEY SOPER

CONTENTS

EPISTLE TO THE SKEPTICS

Why Skepticism Is a Necessity

WE NORMALLY THINK of the struggle with skepticism as an affair only of later adolescence—that mature adults and little children have nothing to do with it. Clearly this view leaves out of account the actual situation —the intellectual climate—which surrounds and confronts the child, which challenges him to affirmative or negative response, and eventually thrusts him into the adolescent turmoil of the mind.

My own story, in no sense normative, is simply a case in point.

A Childhood Experience

No one knows whether the sons of ministers are uniquely blessed or cursed. A high percentage, in fact, have achieved positions of leadership, but they may well have been irritated into eminence. The sons of laymen have problems of their own. If the problem of a minister's son is peculiar, to say the least, the problem of a Methodist minister's son is more so. Further, the problem of a fundamentalist Methodist minister's son is most peculiar of all. Unquestionably the situation possesses advantages as well as disadvantages. There is not much breadth to the experience, but in a particularly straightened way there is considerable

depth. One becomes aware of God, of meaning and purpose, more painfully than joyfully, before he is aware
either of the city in which he lives or of the wider world
beyond it. The God to whom he is thus forcefully intro-
duced is a real being, not the less real because essentially
finite. The fundamentalist's God is a great and terrible
Lord—not unlike Louis XIV or Henry VIII, as they must
have appeared to the children of their day—an enormous
man, a specific being, a finite reality; he does have something to do with the lives of ordinary men, but in the
main he is above and beyond the mundane world and essentially at war with it. The God who is the life in all that
lives, the existence in all that exists, as well as the love
that directs all life and all existence toward universal freedom and faithfulness in fellowship—this God is not perceived at all. God, as understood by the child of a fundamentalist Methodist minister, seems often filled with un-
accountable wrath; one should always be on the right side
of God, but which is his right side? There is no such thing
as safety or security. From the wrath of such a God, and
from such a God, as Nels F. S. Ferré has understood, a
child can wish for nothing but escape. The problem is
further complicated: God, as perceived by the fundamentalist third of Methodism, is tremendously exercised
against smoking, drinking, playing cards, and dancing; he
seems concerned only secondarily if at all with justice or
injustice in government, with race discrimination, class
prejudice, war and poverty, physical illness and mental
frustration. Human development, as such, is outside the
divine interest; the sole objective is the salvation in another world of a submissive minority; the promised paradise offers only such joy as can be found in absolute and
unthinking obedience. To inquire whether what is taught
about God is true is to be damned, in this world and the
next. The stubborn majority are destined, if not predestined, to hell's flaming cauldron forever. The "saved,"

who have submitted to the unexamined faith of fundamentalism, must try to take others with them into the
wholesome Methodist paradise, but there is no reason for
the hope that more than a few will be "saved."

All this was taught me, essentially if not exactly in the
form I have described, from the moment I was conscious
of anyone or anything about me. The result, if the present
estimate is accurate, was a high degree of immunization
against religion, against ethics, against skepticism, and
very nearly against life.

Immunization did not occur overnight, yet was real
enough—in all the areas I have mentioned. Religion required me to pray when I went to bed, to attend church
Sunday morning and evening, to recite verses at Junior
League every Sunday afternoon, to behave in Sunday
school every Sunday morning, to sing hymns and listen to
testimonies every Wednesday night. Religion required me
to be called a "sissy" by my classmates at public school. I
was never to fight, not even to defend myself. Religion
required me not to attend movies, not even westerns. In
high school, religion required me not to attend dances,
not to put my arm around a girl, not to think "sensual"
thoughts. Family peace was the reward of full obedience
to these "heavenly" visions; personal sorrow, the reward
of nonconformity. Simple protective self-interest taught
me to play along with these precepts, the only ones I
knew, but my heart was not in them. Now and then I de-
lighted my mother by learning and reciting long passages
from the Bible or by offering what sounded like a very
mature prayer. Simple terror of my parents and of God,
who seemed very much like them, seized me—after but
not before each disobedience. I was fully churched, but
not even slightly interested in religion. I was successfully
inoculated against it.

My adaptation to fundamentalist Methodist ethics was
similar. The sheer weight of ethical responsibility, as I

conceived it, was too much for my ability. Not inwardly conformed to the prescribed rule, I was either prudent or in trouble. Presently I developed a double standard—as a necessity of survival. I resolved firmly to conform in word and deed, but privately to do as I pleased, when no one seemed to be looking. Shortly thereafter, my father received long, threatening, anonymous letters, urging him to take me in hand. This he frequently did, not less heartily because only for my good. I told my parents I was going to play tennis—an approved activity—but went regularly to the movies. My allowance was small and I decided to augment it—to help myself to things I wanted or to take things simply for the pleasure of "getting away with it." When school was not in session I worked at odd jobs for a handful of employers—and helped myself to funds beyond my pay. Morality, as I had been taught it, seemed beyond my ability, and largely beyond my interest. I simply abandoned the effort to be moral. In fear of the wrath of God, I attempted to hide from him—behind regular church attendance and occasional good deeds. It adds up to this: I was inoculated, successfully, against morality.

I had never heard of skepticism, except as a form of swearing. Now and then I heard rumblings of damnation against persons my parents regarded as "infidels," "atheists," "skeptics," and "freethinkers." No one told me that it was my duty, and my privilege, to try to think for myself, to attempt to separate sense from nonsense. Nor was I equipped to do so. I was immunized against skepticism by an effective, if largely unconscious, inoculation against it. No right-thinking respectable person could be a skeptic; skeptics were simply outside the charmed circle of acceptability.

The Skeptical Task

A childhood experience is hardly adequate as an illustration of the necessity of reason in the struggle toward mature religion, if it were not for the fact that every man among us began as a child; that unless the child is understood, the man cannot be; that my own relation to the skeptical task began in childhood; and finally that we all are closer to children than we think.

Some time ago I received a letter from a woman, a vigorous enemy of religion as she understood it. She ended her letter: "Yours for truth and sanity." In content the letter likewise gloried in the true and the sane. This woman rightly recognized a simple but far-reaching principle: *truth and sanity make skepticism a perpetual necessity*. There is never too much skepticism in the world, but always too little—and often too late. Religion suffers not from an intelligent skepticism, but from the lack of it. As Reinhold Niebuhr has understood, the world is so full of bunkum that one must be perpetually on guard lest he receive as truth all sorts of falsehood, lest he swallow as food all kinds of poison. *Skepticism is neither more nor less than man's necessary effort to distinguish between sense and nonsense in every dimension of his world.* Skepticism, thus defined, is more than a human requirement. God himself demands it; for God is much more of an unbeliever than is any atheist. He does not believe at all, not even a little bit, in the false gods we prefer to him—our man-made gods of race and class, of nation and creed. When men refuse to be skeptical, as God is skeptical, bigotry, hypocrisy, and cruelty cripple human life and enslave the human spirit. When men refuse to be skeptical, the insane dethrones sanity—in politics, in economics, in race relations, and in ethical standards: therefore in the one thing that involves everything, religion. For *religion is devotion*—to whatever a man regards as worthy of it, and whether in or out of church. The devotion, not of his lips but of his life, is the actual content of every man's religion. True religion, on any showing, is devotion to what is true. Hence the perpetual necessity of separating truth from falsehood in religious belief and practice; the task is a sacred one, for it is the task of God.

The wonder is not that there are many unbelievers in religion but that there are few. Religious unbelievers reject the claim of particular religious organizations that they speak infallibly for God. In this sense God himself is surely a religious unbeliever; he finds something of himself in each religion; he finds himself fully in none. It is therefore God himself who requires the rejection of the false, but also the acceptance and support of the true. Only a man who values the true can reject the false; only he has a basis of rejection. The discovery, acceptance, and support of what is permanently and universally true—this, after all, is the central concern of religion.

Conflicting religious ideas and organizations today demand allegiance. The sifting assignment is never an easy one. If we retreat from the magnitude of the task, we have withdrawn from the battle to make reason prevail in institutions and men. The moment we withdraw from the battle we cease to be skeptical, as God is; we have chosen capitulation and cowardice; we have declared in our hearts that no distinction exists between reason and unreason. There is no honorable escape: we must remain alert, determined to distinguish the real from what is said to be real; we must give our strength of mind and hand to what we see to be true, pending clearer sight, or cease to be men.

What then, in simple description, are a few of the religious alternatives now before us?

Hinduism, a modern religion, is closely bound up with the life of India. Its attention is focused upon eternity; it therefore tends to leave unchanged and unchallenged a caste system which places the human spirit in a strait jacket; the caste system itself is sanctified as the yoke of God, the burden of *karma.*

One can only sympathize with Nehru's contention that

the basic need of modern India is a century of atheism, for the Hindu idea of God and the Hindu caste system seem to stand or fall together. India believes in a thousand gods, in three gods, in no god, in an ultimate unconscious and purposeless Brahman, but in all its belief ignores man as he is in this space-time universe. It tends to sanctify what is, and thus prevents the coming of what ought to be. If Hinduism is the only religion available to man, it is possible that man cannot afford religion. Any religious preoccupation which excludes the better and more in this world—for all men—seems a form of blasphemy wearing the robes of piety.

Genuine saints, however defined, exist in any and every religion. *Buddhism* too has its human channels of blessing. Yet the original Buddhist teaching, whether in Hinayana or Mahayana form, urges the cessation of human desire, including the desire for progress, the desire for salvation. The simplicity of Buddhism, beneath its accumulated layers of ritual and doctrine, is not the least of its attractions. Every man can begin where he is, and labor toward the full extinction of desire. The complete annihilation of defensive self-interest, which prefers its own good to the common good, is a virtue; the destruction of interest in the common good, which includes the good of the self, is a vice—no matter how religious its disguise. The extinction of self-centered love is good, but only when it is replaced or displaced by the positive love of all men and the common good. Truth demands, and rewards, wholehearted devotion—in religion as in science—not the extinction of the desire for the better and the more. Sanity demands that selfhood be respected, not annihilated; cultivated, not destroyed; strengthened, not weakened. To seek one's own true good is what Christianity calls charity; one cannot seek another's true good unless he seeks also his own. To seek one's own true good *against* the common good is the cancer of self-centered love. To seek the common good, which includes one's own good, is always moral and everywhere relevant.

The Protestant Reformation began when John Huss, Savonarola, John Wycliffe, and Martin Luther became skeptical, as God is. They found the courage to subject the *Roman claim of absolute dominion* over the minds of men to honest scrutiny. The reformers rejected not Roman Christianity but the Roman assumption that the pope and God, for all practical purposes, were coterminous, the assumption that the directives of the Roman hierarchy were identical with God's will. If a subversive is one who does not identify the will of God with the will of the party in power, the reformers were subversives. They questioned prevailing opinion; as subversives they were hounded to their death. It was the purpose of the reformers to release the discerning love which God is, and requires, from its imprisonment within the empire of the heirs of Caesar.

Modern Roman Catholicism offers the world an avenue of prayer and a source of power, but also an absolute authority in matters of faith and morals. Dostoevsky insisted that Rome has uniformly accepted the sword which Christ rejected in the third temptation; it persuades when it must, coerces when it can; it is Thomas Aquinas in America, the Grand Inquisitor in Spain. The ritual of the priest is a form of prayer; the humble heart prays through any form of prayer, and is heard. The mistake of the priest is this: he considers that his ritual monopolizes the love of God. There is no recognition in the Roman Church that "think we must, but never confuse or equate or identify our thinking with God's." As Paul Tillich has repeatedly insisted, when a human institution claims divine dignity, divine infallibility, and, unlike divinity, demands the surrender of freedom, it becomes demonic—an obstruction to spiritual growth. It claims to know the real, the true, and the sane with absolute certainty; it thus claims more than it knows, demands an absolute surrender that belongs only to God. Rational integrity, the demand of God, is bypassed or denied. To the extent that Rome considers its truth and its life above criticism, it is, as the reformers called it, a form of idolatry, an obstacle to the growth in man of the image of God. To be sure, stone walls do not a prison make, nor iron bars a cage—to those who are happy behind them. God hears prayer and creates saints in the Roman as in other churches; when God creates critics of human idolatry, in any religious system, the critic may find that the way of the transgressor is hard.

The essential Protestant theme was, and remains, the first commandment: "Thou shalt have no other gods before me" (Exodus 20:3). No human knowledge of God is to be equated with God's knowledge of himself. The claim of absolute infallibility—especially in matters of faith and morals—by any human institution or person, however holy, is the end of growth toward one world of freedom and faithfulness in fellowship, the only intelligible goal of history. Infallible truth is frozen truth, and frozen truth cannot grow. Infallibility belongs to God alone, and in God infallibility is not frozen.

The Protestant mind, at the beginning, was skeptical; it is Protestant only when it remains so. Protestant dogmatism has in part neutralized the immense gain that Protestantism offered the world. Protestantism, which began as the democracy of Christianity, has become, on the surface, a community of competing infallibilities; it is ripe for the scythe of the skeptic, for the new Reformation. The World Council of Churches, now attempting wholeheartedly to make one faith of many fragments, is the new Martin Luther, the new Erasmus—and the stronger because it unites the strength of the one with the serenity of the other. The Roman Church equates its papal pronouncements on faith and morals with divinity; Protestantism first equated the Bible, then the current conclusions of human reason, with the voice of God. In either case, a

basic truth is overlooked. Nothing human is above criticism; nothing human is above the necessity of analysis;
nothing human is exempt from judgment. Protestantism
cannot afford *not* to be scrutinized. When the Protestant
and the skeptic part company, Protestantism is judged and
found wanting by the Protestant principle—that only God
is infallible.

Truth and sanity are too important, too necessary, to be
taken for granted or encrusted with tradition; now as always, they await release in the house of bondage. The task
of the skeptic seems irreligious but is most deeply religious; seems secular but is intrinsically sacred. Protestantism is torn, humiliated, ravaged, but not destroyed by a
variety of false absolutes called salvation by total immersion, salvation by prohibition, salvation by "right" doctrine, salvation by "apostolic succession," salvation by the
present achievements of human reason. Our plague of
Protestant distortions is not good enough for man. God is
more than our grasp of him; it is he who grasps us. He participates, with compassion, in our absurdities, and sustains
us in the midst of our distortions; he never abandons his
native priority to our conclusions.

Skepticism is a costly necessity, for skeptics make mistakes like other men. They have been known to throw out
the baby with the bathwater, to cast away faith with folly,
character with its caricatures. But skepticism, by definition, is skeptical of all "closed" seeing, including its own.

When the skeptic ceases to work, growth is dead, and
with it, hope. It is just our old neighbor, God, who keeps
the skeptic working and will never let him rest.

Pre-Skeptical Religion

EACH PHASE in my own experience illustrates in its own way the inadequacy of religion without skepticism, and the inadequacy of skepticism without religion. At the first phase of my life I attempted to do without both—to live with neither breadth nor depth. Life itself thrust me beyond mere existence, forced me to the search for meaningful questions and relevant answers.

The Beginning of Serious Religion

At the first stage in my experience, skepticism was clearly excluded and as clearly needed. At the second stage, religious seriousness broke through to me, but the absence of faithful skepticism made inadequate religion inevitable. Evangelists threw the fear of God into me—aided by a youth's sensitive imagination. Often in the past I had made the journey to the mourner's bench, and hoped for the best. Precious little had ever come of it. A few weeks after each evangelist's departure I was back in the double standard. Inward conformity is not easily achieved; the human spirit is structurally opposed to it. You can get any man to conform outwardly—if the pressure is great enough; no one can conform in mind and soul without his own consent. Two events resulted in my "conversion." A particularly effective evangelist, a young man with a quiet voice, convinced me that I must stop stealing from my employers and deceiving my parents. I confessed my sins to my father with fear and trembling. I asked him to loan me the money to make restitution to the people I had robbed, and to forgive my frequent lies and deceits. All this he was willing to do. Fundamentalists are not by nature ungenerous or unkind, though doctrine sometimes makes them so. Early the following morning, with red face, I walked round the town, like a mailman or a paymaster, distributing checks and making explanations. Many were surprised; all were willing to forgive and forget; some expressed admiration. One was not surprised, but pleased that my restitution had preceded by a day his planned report to the police. In a year or so I repaid my father's loan.

Simple fear of consequences had something to do with this experience. In itself it would not have produced inward conformity. During the following year I was increasingly conformist in every way I knew, but I was something less than happy. I had cleared the sanctuary of my soul of accumulated debris, but the room was empty and cold. A year or so later my parents took me with them to the rip-roaring summer camp meetings they seemed to enjoy. The singing was unforgettable—seldom equaled in the walk-in refrigerator churches. People became ecstatic in their consciousness of the grace of God. And the meals were good. There were other young people about; some seemed almost human. But the preaching and the altar services were a torture to my soul. I learned that it was not enough to conform to the fundamentalist moral standard, not even inwardly. One must know in his heart that he was "saved," that God had given him peace, had written his name in the Lamb's Book of Life, that heaven was certain and sure. One could then shout for joy. After a few weeks the idea took hold. I learned that I must *trust*

God, who had sent his Son to die for me; I must *believe* that I was accepted; I must accept my acceptance and rejoice in it. This I decided to do; at once the promised peace and joy entered my soul. I knew at last that I was redeemed, washed in the blood of the Lamb.

I was inwardly integrated; the double standard was gone; I had no desire to disobey. Revolt had been drained from my heart. I was at peace with God and man. The long war was over. I could never work up much of a shout, as a proper Methodist, but I did rejoice that I had found the way. I could sing and laugh. For the first time in my life I enjoyed the company of religious people—the more religious the better. Gone was all desire to smoke, to go to the movies, and to dance. Prayer meetings became a special delight; I gave my testimony as one of the group, an accepted member of the family of Christ.

People started to trust me—a new experience. At school the teachers treated me with respect. My fellow students, strangely enough, no longer sneered at me; they respected and accepted me; they considered that I was narrow but sincere, a very trustworthy person. It was good to be approved by my classmates, and often elected to responsible school jobs.

A famous Bible teacher visited our church for two weeks. His strong masculine personality completely overwhelmed me. Within a few months I became a Bible expositor and memorized vast passages of Scripture. I started to preach, and was exhilarated by the sympathetic response of the people. I felt increasingly competent as an interpreter of the Bible and considered myself a promising young fundamentalist Bible teacher. With sincere good will, the vigorous leader advised me not to attend college but to hole up somewhere with the Bible for two or three years, as he had done. My father, who had worked his way through Syracuse University, valued an education. At his insistence I went to college, but decided to learn as little as possible; I would merely secure the proper degrees to ensure respectful attention to my Bible teaching. I learned nothing in college but managed passing grades. However, I climbed out of bed every morning at five to study the Bible, and wrote and published—at my own expense— several gospel tracts. My first book, *Studies in Romans*, published at this time, contained a mass of undigested biblical expositions, exegetically doubtful and wholly premature. The sales, however, financed one year in college.

My experience of "grace" proved a mixed blessing. I developed a considerable pride in my spiritual maturity, my biblical knowledge, my separateness from the lesser breed without the law. And in time biology played bull-in-the-ring with my theology. I found I could think my way round absolute Methodist morality. Quite unintentionally, the Apostle Paul proved an unexpected ally. "Every sin is without the body," he said (I Corinthians 6:18). In my misinterpretation, I could do anything I wished to do —so long as I willed only good from the experience. This simple casuistry (described to a T by Pascal in his *Provincial Letters)* opened the door to biology, and biology entered with a bang. I was a small-size religious prig and a full-size hypocrite; it was altogether necessary that reality, truth, and sanity crack open my pious and smelly little soul—to make room for healthier growth.

The Break-through of God

Many men have experienced, in one way or another, an adolescent commitment to inadequate religion. It is often characterized by sincerity, even by humility—yet it enjoys no real depth nor breadth. Its God is too small; its understanding of reality is too limited. It is sufficient for a brief period until it is presented with a radical demand for growth. It is possible that some men, engaged in demanding daily tasks, may never experience a radical call to growth beyond an initial emotional adjustment to reality.

The difficulty is simple and obvious for most of us: when reality begins to break through our small and inadequate world, it finds no convenient place to stop. Our defenses against reality come tumbling down. Either the world or our insufficient conception of it must give ground; either God or our too meager understanding of him must yield. It is clear that the contest is unequal; our china teacup cannot hold the ocean.

In no human situation can God (the religious term for Reality) be wholly prevented from active operation for human good. Whether we are saints or sinners, missionaries or atheists, God is within us and around us from the hour of our birth, and long before the hour of our conception. Our constant human dilemma is the choice between creativity and cowardice—to labor with God for human good or to sacrifice human good on the altar of our own race, class, or creed. Whether we choose the harder right or the easier wrong, our freedom is respected and sustained within a context of responsibility. God surrounds us, judges us, summons us to growth; we are guests in his house, children called to maturity. God always bestows on us more than he receives.

In three definable ways God continuously acts for human good: he sustains the world without and the world within us; he corrects our misuse or perversion of freedom, whether we act together or alone; he directs our half-finished world and our half-finished souls toward fulfillment. Often enough we resist the creative enterprise—the creation of one world—but we can prevent neither the work of God nor the final achievement of his purpose. The work of God cannot be prevented; he sustains existence itself, resists its distortion or perversion, and directs our scattering and shattering fragments toward fellowship. The final achievement of his purpose cannot be prevented; whole-family fellowship—the goal of history—is his nature and demand, while all power is his on earth and in heaven. The strength which sustains our freedom is sufficient to teach freedom faithfulness to the common good.

From God comes not only our courage, correction, and direction but also our creativity. By definition, God (or Reality) is the life in all that lives, the existence in all that exists; he is also the light which makes all life and all existence intelligible. Our courage to be, to struggle, to surmount obstacles, to increase our knowledge, our skill, our usefulness—this courage is God's gift; it is God at work within us, the push of power, the energy of mind and hand.

We all receive, whether or not we accept, correction. God continually separates the false from the true in all men, that the true may prevail. When we worship false gods, God eventually destroys them—lest they destroy us. The corrective action of reality operates only for human good—not always for "imagined" good. No punishment at the time seems to be joyous; nonetheless, it yields the fruit of faithfulness in them who are exercised thereby. All men, nations, cultures, and religions, must, at times, be "reduced to English"—for their own survival and growth; all receive occasionally, and if anything with excessive moderation, the creative grace of real correction. Creativity is courage plus accepted correction.

Courage and correction together direct us on our way. Wise or foolish, rich or poor, scientists or fundamentalists, we all receive continuously the gift of direction, whether or not we are aware of it, whether or not we heed it.

When we are deeply committed to the common good we receive something more than courage, correction, and direction; we receive the gift of creativity, what Christians call "the baptism of the Holy Spirit." Light directly enters the life open to receive it. All men, in some degree, are creative, through the common gifts of courage, correction, and direction. Special creativity, the ability to accomplish the good, seems to be a unique gift of God to receptive civilizations and men. Whether special creativity is a special or general gift, it lends no support to self-righteousness. Men and nations with unique abilities and unique tasks do not possess creativity; creativity possesses them. The goodness that sustains, corrects, and directs us is greater than our righteousness as well as greater than our sin. We can never justify ourselves nor feel that we have achieved the good. The good that we seem to do is not our gift to God but his gift to us, and to the world—through, and in spite of, our best and our worst.

Finally, to all men, and specially to those who love and seek the good, God is more than courage, correction, direction, and creativity; he is the crown of life, the reward of faithfulness: his purpose, not destined to fail, is the goal of evolution and history. Because we are grasped and called by all-powerful Good, the future is greater and richer than the present—in every dimension of thought and life. God is before us; God is with us and in us; and God is perpetually beyond us. His will shall prevail on earth, for the good which sustains and directs our freedom is stronger than all its distortions or perversions; man and the world will one day bear the unmistakable image of God.

Whether we are atheists or theists, we live from first to last within the sustaining, correcting, and directing hand of God; our finest creativity is his presence and power acting for good within us and upon us. He is our reward; his purpose of human brotherhood is our highest good.

God breaks through into every system of thought. Children, and men with the minds of children, receive his gifts of courage, correction, and direction. If they will, they receive also his gift of creativity; whether they will or no, his will is their goal, their impossible but imperative demand. Literate men, and men who have added love to literacy, likewise live within his surrounding and controlling presence. He breaks through into history specially in heroes, martyrs, and saints; but as courage, correction, and

direction, he breaks through in saints and sinners alike.
God is greater than all our thought—whether pre-skeptical,
skeptical, or post-skeptical; he is greater than all our faith
—whether profound or superficial; he is greater than all
our maturity, which is always premature, better than all
our virtue, truer than all our truth. For this reason we
say: where reality is, God is.

God Is Greater than Our Understanding

When one stops to think about it, our faith, our thought,
our knowledge, and our opinion are not four things but
one. All are less than the truth they seek to comprehend,
less than the whole of reality. What we think is what we
believe; what we believe is what we think; and as we
think, we act. What we claim to know is neither more nor
less than our opinion.

Distinctions can be multiplied between whole-thinking
and part-thinking, between nominal and actual beliefs,
between disciplined and undisciplined knowledge, between informed and uninformed opinion. Yet, after these
distinctions are made, God is greater than our whole-
thinking and not identical with it, greater than our actual
beliefs and not fully pictured by them, greater than our
disciplined knowledge and not imprisoned therein, greater
than our informed opinion and discontinuous with it. A
great gulf is fixed between faith, thought, knowledge, and
opinion that have cost nothing and are worth what they
cost, and faith, thought, knowledge, and opinion that have
struggled with blood, sweat, and tears to pay the price of
sight. Across the chasm from cheap to costly faith, from
shallow to profound thought, from nonsense to tested
knowledge, from wishful opiate to wistful opinion, is
built the bridge of sighs, the ordeal of patience and per-
spiration, the agony of the struggle to see. Yet the most
costly faith, the profoundest thought, the most accurate
knowledge, and the best informed opinion are one and

the same in this: they do not fully grasp God; it is God who grasps them.

As Kierkegaard understood, when we do not know that our best representation of God is only an approximation, we actually misrepresent him. Omniscience is not in our possession; it is not in our faith, our thought, our knowledge, whether scientific or religious; it is not in our opinion. As Cromwell put it to the Covenanters, convinced of their infallibility: "I ask you, gentlemen, before Almighty God, to consider that you may be mistaken."

It is nonetheless our human glory that our faith, thought, knowledge, and opinion participate in the truth which God is and requires. Though a fool, the wayfaring man cannot wholly miss some aspect of truth. Though a saint, the wisest man cannot wholly escape some aspect of error. God is humble enough to lend himself to our distorted faith, our deceptive thought, our relative knowledge, and our fallible opinion. All men participate in some degree in truth; no man participates fully. We are all summoned to participate as fully as we can, and more fully than we do. God who summons us to better participation is not wholly alien to us: he lives in our lives; he is both the strength and the weakness of our errors.

The opinion we hold nominally, on the top of our minds, is one thing; the opinion we hold actually, in the bottom of our hearts, may be another. The difference is vast between the faith to which we stand as onlookers and the faith to which we stand as disciples. The difference is immeasurable between what we think we think and what we think in action. The difference is cosmic between the knowledge we manipulate and the knowledge that manipulates us. The difference is drastic between the opinion we hold as dilettantes and the opinion that holds us in total commitment. However, both the just and the unjust live by whatever faith, thought, knowledge, and opinion they have in fact. Whatever our faith, thought, knowledge, or opinion, we are stuck with it, and God is not in our possession; he possesses us.

The words—faith, thought, knowledge, opinion—are four symbols for our *conditioned* grasp of the reality which grasps us *unconditionally*.

It does not follow that we should stop thinking; rather, that we should begin to pay the price of sight, to commit ourselves faithfully to what we see to be true, to exercise our critical faculties to separate the true from the false, to realize—with tolerance for other views and critical examination of our own—that what many men see together may better approximate the nature and demand of God than what any man sees alone, yet that what all men see together is less than the truth which waits to be seen.

The Necessity of Commitment

Pre-skeptical religion undoubtedly experiences, in some degree, the break-through of God. Reality does not withhold truth and sanity from children and babes, nor from adults whose minds are twelve years old. Immature prayer, for example, is the attempt to manipulate reality for selfish ends; mature prayer is the surrender of selfish ends to reality. Intercessory prayer is a form of love in action; love always encloses need within a circle of supply. In any form of prayer, reality in some measure breaks through. Prayer may be the simplest form of speech. The cry of a newborn babe is a species of prayer, and the universe is built to answer it. The wisest adult is pre-literate in some dimension of his existence; he may be a doctor of philosophy, but less than a moron in managing a modern mechanism—for example, a motor car. All human development is streaky. All of us are overdeveloped in some areas, underdeveloped in others. Philosophers usually need wives to keep them in touch with reality.

We are all pre-skeptical in some dimension of our knowledge. Division of labor means that we accept our responsibility to be more than pre-literate in our specialized task, and to thank God that some men are willing to be more than pre-literate in other areas of necessity.

A pre-critical or pre-skeptical encounter with God possesses values of its own. The American theologian, Nels F. S. Ferré, has described his three stages of development. He was converted when twelve years old to what he calls traditional Christianity; he accepted the imposed past on his parents' terms, yet, he insists, *not without a direct experience of God.* Next, he passed through a painful period of questioning; he discovered that not every picture of God, even in the Bible, is morally respectable. It occurred to him that Christianity, though wonderful, might not be true. High school and college provided constant assaults upon his pre-skeptical piety. Hard facts, or facts believed to be hard, which may or may not have been as hard as they looked, shattered his bright acceptance of fundamentalist faith. One night, a disillusioned college junior, he knelt down beside his bed, and prayed with tears: "God, if there be any God to hear me, give me at least the courage to be honest" *(The Third Conversion Never Fails,* in David Wesley Soper, editor, *These Found the Way.* Philadelphia: Westminster Press, 1951, p. 133). For a time honesty and Christianity, as he understood them, maintained separate residences. The agony of "advanced" education shattered his inadequate world and brought him to his knees in humility. It is reasonably obvious that at any stage in growth God prefers humility to arrogance, honesty to hypocrisy; that honesty and piety are not two things but one.

Some time later, with help from older and wiser men, Ferré discovered that honesty and Christianity are not enemies but friends. He reached what he calls "post-critical faith"—which is not as post-critical as it seems—through the wilderness of mental anguish, and nine years of physical suffering as a chronic arthritic. "Post-critical faith" is not post-critical in the sense that honesty has been left behind; it accepts the fact that honesty is a divine requirement, that the honesty of God is prior to and greater than, yet also the strength of, all human honesty.

In Ferré's experience, the pre-skeptical faith could not be held into adult years without hypocrisy on the one hand or revision on the other. Perhaps the thrust of criticism into the sacred domain of theology has characterized the spiritual and intellectual histories of doctors of philosophy more than other folk, for the attempt to understand truth is their specialization. Laymen in this sense include all men who are not engaged in the philosophical or theological struggle. For example, it is often strangely true that advanced physical scientists are fundamentalists in religion. On second thought, this fact is not strange at all, for these men are professionals in science but laymen in theology. Perhaps laymen are, and will always be, wholesomely pre-skeptical in their faith. Unfortunately, or rather fortunately, church leaders cannot bank on the permanent ignorance of their congregations, nor forever maintain the comfortable *status quo*. Laymen in every congregation can sometimes distinguish sense from nonsense. In any case, leaders should lead a part of the time, and not be followers only. Their assignment from God, whatever their orders from denominational headquarters, is to become men of sight, able to lead others attempting to see—not the blind who lead or the blind who follow.

No one, I think, really knows whether it is normal or subnormal for humans to pass from the pre-skeptical A to the post-skeptical C through the painfully skeptical B. To many, at least, this experience of the divine break-through has been a necessity. We have started out as parasites on our parents' religion, as we were parasites inevitably on their economic resources, yet we were not without some experience of growing responsibility. There is nothing evil, so far as I know, in the fact that English-speaking parents raise English-speaking children. It is not, in my opinion, a form of paternalist imperialism that parents give their children whatever culture they have received and shaped, including their religion, their encounter with God, their experience of reality.

Adolescence often seems a form of insanity; it is more accurately described as immaturity. A normal adolescent wishes to stand on his own feet—economically, spiritually, intellectually—and must do so to become an adult, an individual, a self. Until he becomes a self, he has very little self to place in the service of God; only a self-determining self can become a son, a brother, and a saint. Original sin, the excessive assertion of selfhood, is thus an original necessity. God thrusts us forward, and summons us onward, first to selfhood and then to brotherhood. We pass through the pedagogy of excessive self-assertion in order that we may have and be selves who accept the responsibility of freedom and faithfulness in fellowship. To some extent, during our painful transition, our wilderness, our groping toward selfhood and self-direction, we revolt against all authority human and divine; we try our strength against other strength to discover what our strength is. God grasps us, breaks through to us, in the midst of our immaturity.

At the third stage, if we are not wide awake, we pass—all too prematurely—from the transitional B to the post-skeptical C. Our actual objective is not post-skepticism, but the full recognition of skepticism as the critic and ally of faith. Commitment after criticism can be as deadly as commitment before criticism; the need is to keep criticism and commitment at work, freely and faithfully together. Nevertheless, at the third stage, the lonely anguish of revolt rediscovers the human race. To our surprise and pleasure we find ourselves surrounded with humans not wholly hostile; we begin to discover that the God we have rejected is greater than our rejection, has accepted and sustained us in the midst of our revolt, is great enough to seek our good in, through, and beyond our heroic effort to "go it alone." We are startled to discover that God, despite our awkwardness and waywardness, is not against us but for us.

It is not wholly evil, though not wholly good, that we fail often enough to distinguish divinity from dust—in ourselves, in the Bible, and in our national culture. We walk before we run; our commitment to inadequate ideas maintains our sanity, our continuity with our own past, till better ideas are formed within us, and sanity itself, which is continuity with God, makes us increasingly creative. Yet commitment without criticism is commitment unexamined and uncontested; it is more or less adequate for children, and for adults in technology who are children in theology; it experiences the break-through of God in courage, correction, direction, and even in creativity. It becomes the enemy of man when it retreats from growth, when it sets its face against the call of God to launch out into the deep.

The Hazard of Commitment

There is very little point in separating wheat from chaff if you are not going to make wheat into bread. Faith is commitment to what one sees to be true; criticism is the necessary effort, however arduous, to separate what is true from what is false—that the true may prevail. True answers demand a questioning spirit or they remain undiscovered; they then demand an adventuring spirit or they remain unapplied. When convincing answers are found, integrity of mind demands commitment to them—pending better light. Better light cannot come unless we walk in the light that is given. Our practical certainty must be put to the test—in the broad field of action as well as in the high tower of thought.

Criticism wholly allergic to commitment shrinks into cowardice. We live, whether atheists or saints, by what we think. It is a matter of life or death that we think as accurately as we can, with all the help we can get; to divorce criticism from commitment is to separate wheat from chaff only to throw the wheat away; we thus lose the ability to distinguish one from the other. However limited our sight, we must live by what we see to be true, or the humanity and the heroism die out of us.

Unless criticism and commitment are allies, we get nowhere in our understanding of God. The builder must remain endlessly alert to separate what is inadequate from what is adequate—in blueprint, in material, in procedure —or the building will fall. But adequacy in blueprint and adequacy in material are themselves inadequate without the follow-through of actual construction. Actual construction will necessitate changes in blueprint, material, and procedure. Not to build, when material and blueprint are in hand, is to be a dilettante.

The hazard of commitment without criticism is suggested in the following statement: "Begin with certainties and you end up with doubts; begin with doubts and you end up with certainties." The statement is not wholly true; without tentative certainties, one does not begin at all. Yet the statement contains a helpful insight into our human predicament. Young people, nurtured at home on pious certainties, are frequently turned inside out as college freshmen or sophomores. Uncertainty becomes the campus creed. As William Crary Brownell put it: "We considered ourselves emancipated, but were only unbuttoned." Juniors and seniors are often uncertain of uncertainty as the infallible faith; the more timid retreat to prefreshman certainties; others remain in a prolonged tension of doubt; still others ignore the issue altogether and go forth to sell bonds—to the sound of trumpets; but not a few press forward to skepticism's creative alliance with serious faith.

Criticism becomes uncreative when divorced, in principle or in practice, from commitment. "There lives more faith in honest doubt than in half the creeds." These words, attributed to Alfred Lord Tennyson, are often misunderstood. To become a man of doubt, to dissolve all commitments, to live by criticism alone, to espouse no cause, to place one's strength in the service of no enterprise, is to become, in fact, a vegetative nonentity. To live as a man is to live by commitment; yet we cannot live well without criticism. Commitment is synthesis; criticism is analysis. The first integrates, the second separates; the one concludes, the other scrutinizes. Always the human task is not to escape from doubt, but with the help of doubt to become more than a vegetative nonentity. As Aldous Huxley has understood: "There is more doubt in honest faith than in all the writings of the atheists." *Honest* faith is always self-critical; as G. K. Chesterton knew, the church has had to be careful—if only that the world might be careless. Reasoning *faith,* in H. Richard Neibuhr's view, has a future, while reasoning *faithlessness* has neither a future nor a past.

Criticism of the false without commitment to the true is paralysis of mind and lethargy of spirit. If commitment without criticism is fanaticism, criticism without commitment is futility. Creative personalities are sometimes considered fanatics, until their contribution is understood and appropriated; they are never dilettantes, never cowards, never apostles of futility. Truth and sanity are too important, too necessary, to be lost by default. Reality is the pearl of great price; creative souls will sell all they have to obtain it. Creativity breaks through all the time and in all dimensions, but its healing operation in society and the soul is more often prevented by dilettantism than by high seriousness. If the assumption of infallibility, of ultimate finality, is thrilling but destructive among fanatics, it is both enervating and destructive among the apostles of futility. The view that no truth is worth personal commitment dissolves all loyalties—even loyalty to self.

Criticism without commitment is window-shopping, an examination of what is offered for sale accompanied by a firm determination not to buy. It is an act of piety to say: "I refuse to buy what is not worth the price." It is an act of final frustration, of self-betrayal, to say: "What is offered is worth any price, but my life motto is 'buy nothing.' "

Evangelical atheists, as anxious as the Apostle Paul to convert the world, are a painful disturbance to unexamined faith, but they are more admirable than the merely effeminate who reject the yoke of what they themselves see to be true. Atheistic Communism is not as comfortable to have around as uncommitted effeminacy, but it commands greater respect. If David was a man after God's own heart in his willingness to venture, to risk something for the greater good, devoted atheism is closer to reality than undevoted theism. Religion is *devoted* living; hence the necessity of sorting out the offered objects of devotion. But to analyze the offered objects of devotion and never to put one's strength in the cause of good is not only the end of heroism; it is the end of the world, the atrophy of the will. As T. S. Eliot has understood in *Hollow Men,* the refusal of what is seen to be good brings the world to an end—not with a bang but with a whimper. This spiritual recoil from responsibility, this effeminate evasion of the cost of commitment, this retreat from courage to cowardice, is unreasoning *faithlessness,* beneath all admiration, beneath all contempt. If criticism without commitment is long continued, the mind itself succumbs and creativity is dead.

The Growth of Commitment

Both criticism and commitment exist within the nature and demand of God, and are therefore legitimate activities of human reason. But the question must be asked: "How shall criticism and commitment be related?"

We can no longer accept the view that commitment *excludes* criticism. On that view all questioning of truths declared infallible by popes or dictators is rejected; the questioners, from John Huss to Cardinal Mindszenty, are burned at the stake or murdered in "protective custody." All criticism of truths declared infallible by nationalist hysteria is branded Communism; the critics are summoned before congressional inquisitors and thrown out of their jobs. Jesus pointed out with penetrating sarcasm: it would be a shame if a prophet of the Lord were put to death elsewhere than in the "Holy" City. Commitment which rejects honest criticism is too doubtful to be helpful, whether political or religious. Commitment exists to redeem the world, not to retreat from it or to exclude it; commitment which excludes the world in principle is more worldly than it knows.

We can no longer accept the view that criticism *excludes* commitment—that criticism is an absolute, commitment a relative demand. On that view one's duty is always to question; commitment to what is seen to be true is optional and dispensable. This is the sorrow of life at low pressure, of liberalism that has become soft, has withdrawn from all commanding loyalties—in politics and religion alike. We live by whatever commitment we find convincing; to refuse the right and duty of commitment is to refuse our humanity, to put out the flame of joy in our hearts and the light in our eyes. To commit ourselves and our strength to what we cannot but believe is to open the prison of "attitudinarian" criticism, to transcend effeminacy and egoism.

We can no longer accept the view that commitment exists in an *isolated* compartment above criticism. This view has helped many individuals during trying crises in their lives. They have placed their loyalties in the attic, safely withdrawn from the skeptical struggle. Loyalties are necessities, not luxuries. The effort to separate the false from the true is a necessity also. Great commitment and great criticism must operate together on all floors—neither elevated to the attic nor relegated to the basement. It simply will not do to say: "Truth is so wonderful a treasure that we must use it sparingly." Commitment does not exist solely within and for the church; it must shed its light in and for the world. Criticism is not solely a necessity in the world; in the church also the sub-good must be distinguished from the good. Compartments are helpful in stress and strain; but God is greater than our compartments, and shatters them. God requires whole commitment to truth and sanity on every level of life, and alongside it, whole rejection of evil—that good may prevail. In laymen's terms, commitment is not "for Sundays only" and criticism for "weekdays"; both are seven-day necessities.

We can no longer accept the view that criticism and commitment are eternally at war. God, who is greater than our criticism and greater than our commitment, demands our best in both. Commitment which bears witness to a reality greater than itself must never regard criticism as its implacable foe; criticism, by division of labor, is the challenger and the purifier of commitment, for God's sake. The uncontaminated water of river and brook is stored in tanks and reservoirs; chemists continually test the water to ensure that it is fit to drink. Committed men often call critics pagans, heathen—a lesser breed without the law. Committed men are thus more critically minded than they realize; men of criticism are more committed than they know. Criticism and commitment are not enemies but allies, not opponents but partners. To place criticism in the state, and commitment in the church—or the reverse —is to frustrate both criticism and commitment, to distort both politics and religion. One may indeed serve commitment with the right hand, criticism with the left, and not let the one hand know what the other is doing, but this schizophrenic split, like every other, is uncreative. Criticism and commitment have different tasks to perform within the summons of God to serve the common good. Commitment pursues *complete concern;* criticism pursues *inviolate truth;* neither without the other can do God's creative work. The practice of criticism, of objective examination, exists for the sake of fuller and better commitment; it is not the other way round. It is not for the sake of criticism that we commit ourselves to the real; it is rather for the sake of our nobler commitment that our unreality must be detected and destroyed. Commitment makes criticism possible; criticism makes commitment meaningful. In the common creative enterprise, commitment serves the real by affirmation; criticism serves the real by refusing unreality.

Religion fully skeptical, or skepticism fully religious, recognizes that God demands the criticism of the false for the sake of true commitment. He sustains our hour of participation, corrects our perversion of freedom, directs us toward responsible love in the total family of man, makes us, when we are willing, channels of creativity in the world.

Where a man stands conditions, or determines, what he sees—in science, philosophy, politics, economics, and religion. Where a man stands, in fact or in imagination, is his commitment. Criticism cannot operate from nowhere; it is a task force, a mobile unit, highly maneuverable, but it always proceeds from and returns to a base of supply. The base of supply is a "place to stand," a commitment. Neither criticism nor commitment possesses truth; both bear witness to the truth that possesses all commitment and all criticism; from the base of actual commitment, criticism proceeds to its work. In some degree all faith, thought, knowledge, and opinion bear witness to the reality that summons our half-finished souls to meaningful growth. Every man's religion is his response to the reality he sees; the Christian's religion is his response to the reality he sees in the flesh of Jesus, in whom the Church perceives, in focus, the energy of the world and the purpose of the energy, the fulfillment on its way to all men from the future. Love is God's nature and demand. The enterprise of life is not destined to fail; for God, who sustains, corrects, and directs our freedom, is faithful.

If the focus of faith, in Christianity as in Hinduism, had never been incarnate in a man of flesh and blood, we would still experience—though less clearly—the call to responsibility or love as an absolute demand, because it is the nature of God. But Christians, and non-Christians too (the Moslems, for example), are convinced that the man, Jesus, lived—that he lived in love, that love lived in him, as in no man before or since, that a Church sprang into being to increase creative fellowship, the Holy Spirit, in the institutions and practices of men, till the earth shall be filled with faithful freedom as the waters cover the sea. Whether or not Jesus lived as a solitary embodiment of perfect love, Christians, and all men, since the Crucifixion, have increasingly experienced the call to love as the absolute demand—and gift—of God. World wars and H-bombs in our time increasingly underscore the call. Whether or not Jesus lived, the call has been confirmed; we deny it, or refuse it, to our destruction.

Thousands of years had to pass before ape man was ready to become man. Thousands of years had to pass before God could begin, with Christ on the cross, to make self-centered modern man, who is half ape and half angel, into a full-grown son. Even now the work is only begun. But the seed of the future has been planted firmly and forever among us. Christ's suffering in the Garden and on the cross was the birth pain of God's predestined and inevitable new man in a new world. A few men of the future have already appeared among us; more are on the way. As apes had to give way to self-centered modern man, so self-centered modern man must and will give way to God's sons. The future belongs to them. The sons of the self-centered have no greater future than apes in the world of men. Man did not painlessly emerge as successor to the ape; the sons of God will not painlessly emerge as successors to the self-centered.

Each of us, whatever our terminology or intelligence quotient, is daily confronted with the choice: we can move backward toward the ape or forward toward Christ, toward full responsibility for the well-being of all men. We are not free not to choose. Our lives thus far are the choices we have made, intermingled with the choices others have made; our lives in the future, as nations and as men, will be determined by the choices we now make—together and alone. Our choices are real, with real consequences, yet at every moment we ourselves, and our choices, are in better and stronger hands than our own.

Pre-Skeptical Irreligion

To ME, and not to me only, atheism became a necessary and in part purgative step in my developing religious experience. Religious seriousness itself drove me to, through, and beyond atheism. The battering-ram of reality simply leveled into rubble the ramshackle building I had erected against it. In different words, God cannot be prevented from destroying the inadequate ideas men hold about him—to make room for bigger and better ideas—even at the risk of temporary atheism.

Adolescence is always streaky in its development. Adults, on the average, seem more mature in some areas than in others. It is not possible to explain or to understand all the roads that lead to atheism. One is always wiser after the event. To begin with, demi-theism is much more common than either atheism or theism. Demi-theism is belief in half of God—in the energy of the world but not in its purpose, or in purpose but not in energy.

Ten Years of Atheism

Two main factors are readily discernible in the next stage of my pilgrimage. After considerable preparation I reached the split second of insight, the full moment of revelation, when I became, and knew that I was, an atheist.

The first factor was psychological—a simple desire to do as I pleased. For a thousand reasons I wanted to live in the world as it is, to surrender to temptation if I chose, to discover what was on the other side of the fundamentalist Iron Curtain of acceptable behavior. This factor may have been neither more nor less than curiosity—a necessary probing into the unknown. Quite likely it involved the understandable yearning of a premature moralist for sensual experience. Theologically speaking, there was present a deep human desire to rid myself of the divine "ought" pressing in from all sides upon the soul. In any case, I decided to be irresponsible on principle, after long commitment to a responsibility too narrowly conceived. I surrendered rapturously to the inward push of freedom, cast away the imposed yoke of the past, struck a blow for the dignity of self-determination. No longer would I accept any "ought" thrust upon me ready-made by my betters. I was keen to be myself, to be what I was, to get myself together—to discover reality, truth, and sanity for myself.

The second factor was physiological psychology, firmly accepted after long intellectual struggle. I had read nothing but the Bible for half a dozen years, and I gave myself with joy to dozens of neglected books. I was a junior in college, and at nineteen pastor of my own church—in a suburb of New York City. I was bursting with desire to make a name for myself, to cut a noticeable swath before an admiring public, to gain wide acceptance and approval, to be one with the whole world. I challenged leading New York atheists to public debate, and, frightened to the point of tears, defended my fraying fundamentalism before large audiences, never with clear victory or defeat. Sympathizing atheists occasionally gave me books. Presently I determined to read every atheist book I could find, to understand atheism, to convert atheists to fundamentalist faith.

Before long I was neck deep in physiological psychology. The idea grew in my mind that every man's thoughts and choices and actions are entirely predetermined by the interplay of his heredity and environment, that there is no such thing as free will, and no such thing as responsibility. I became at length convinced that a man can do as he pleases, so far as society will let him. He cannot choose as he pleases; his choices are fixed and settled by omnipotent heredity and environment. The so-called freedom of the soul has nothing to do with it one way or another; the God who demands responsibility does not exist.

One day, with the joy of all new converts, I shouted: "Thank God there is no God." To myself I said: "Whereas I was blind, now I see" (John 9:25). Religion, I concluded, was neither more nor less than the effort of dyspeptic saints to take the fun out of life. With a great sense of release I opened my arms to the world, to any and all encounters with my fellow men, and more particularly with women.

From this development one value began to emerge—a kind of conversion to intellectual honesty, so far as I was capable of it, and in terms of the alternatives as I then understood them. Never again would I accept anything as true unless convinced by my own reason. All so-called authority has since remained subject to close scrutiny, neither to be accepted nor rejected at face value. Unfortunately, at the time, reason convinced me that the universe is indifferent to moral honesty.

I was always enraged when people said to me, "But you're not really an atheist." I was an atheist, and I knew it. I was not an agnostic. An agnostic says, "I don't know." He may then try to find out, whether his search leads to theism or atheism. I had concluded my search; I was an absolute atheist. God did not exist. The only eternal reality was matter in motion. Life was an accident, sometimes happy, sometimes sad, but always purposeless, always expendable. I decided to get all I could out of life, to make pleasure my purpose—since no purpose was structural to reality. I resolved to appear moral, even to appear religious, if thereby I could secure the greater pleasure. Or to be frankly immoral and irreligious, if thereby I could escape the greater pain. There was simply no moral law above and beyond men's moral codes. Moral codes were the attempt of the strong to keep the weak in subjection, or the attempt of men to conquer anxiety by the make-believe of settled habits. To me, once and for all, the only reality was matter in motion; the only ethics, expediency in the service of self-interest.

Obviously, I was not a skeptic, a questioner, but a firm dogmatist. I had the answer.

I considered other people's altruism a good thing; it made my pursuit of self-interest less complicated. I considered one-world constitutional government a good thing, and with great zeal translated the American Constitution into a Constitution for the United Nations of the World. I believed in birth control and taught it from the pulpit on "Mother's Day"; for this and for less admirable reasons I was forced to leave my parish. I was not a Communist; my basic training had omitted a social dimension. I believed in socialism, provided it would not interfere with my personal freedom. I was a pacifist, convinced that wars were caused by economic greed, a thing I deplored for reasons of altruism, though I considered altruism itself a flower without root in reality.

I was a standard garden variety atheist, 1931 vintage, a fundamentalist turned inside out, and I remained one for ten years. During those years one light began to shine, but its full power was then hidden from me—a settled determination to accept as true only what is true indeed, to accept no present "seeing" as final, as equal to the reality which is greater than and prior to all human sight. Through those ten years, however, I was skeptical about everything except my own closed "seeing," my own final and, as I thought, everlasting faith—my dogmatic commitment to atheism and ethical expediency. I had succeeded in making one world out of two; the sacred-secular split no longer existed in the world or in my mind. This split is indeed a blasphemy. But I had destroyed the sacred altogether. Reality, as I conceived it, was deaf, dumb, and blind.

Atheism Is Reaction to Inadequate Religion

What atheism amounts to is this: when men begin to believe in the world, they often cease for a time believing in God. And this is only another way of saying that atheism is a natural and indeed inevitable reaction to inadequate religion. God confronts us not only in the world within us but also in the world around us. If we insist that God confronts us only in the world within us, our religion is inadequate; it leaves out of account the world around us—in which also God lives and moves and has his being. Because we have falsely taught that God moves only in the world within us, men become atheists when they discover with seriousness the world around us, and they can do no other. A false choice is the child of a false dilemma. Atheism ends in theism only when men see that in the world around us as well as in the world within us, God confronts us with his nature, his demand, and his gift.

It is not possible for a sane man's conclusions to bear no resemblance whatever to the real world around him and within him. Even insanity enjoys some grasp of reality. Insane people understand, as a rule, that food is food, and gather without coercion at mealtime. By its very nature, reality is present, at times coercively present, in all human thinking and acting. We possess, enjoy, and abuse a real measure of freedom. We are at liberty to resist or advance the cause of God—in every dimension of our lives; yet God's will remains coercive. If you like, we are "predestined" to exercise our freedom. Through the exercise of freedom we learn what God demands. Through the misuse of freedom we learn what God rejects. Through the right use of freedom we learn what God accepts. God, working through purpose and energy, makes each life, and the whole of life, an educational enterprise. Through long decades God teaches us, as individuals, his demands, guides us to avoid what he rejects, leads us to what he accepts. Through long centuries whole civilizations learn his demands. When civilizations lose a sense of purpose, they collapse of their own weight. Through the rise and fall of civilizations, mankind as a whole slowly but surely learns what God demands, what God rejects, what God accepts. The double thrust of energy and purpose forces man, over many millennia, to cast away untruth and insanity, to surrender himself and his institutions to the real. God has thus far sustained mankind in the pilgrimage—in the midst of the best and the worst. For this reason Christians speak of the "grace of God." The breakdown of civilizations, empires, and souls—what Christians call "judgment"—is an act of God, an act of grace—a teaching or cleansing experience for the human race as a whole. Failure, to those who reject the ingredients of success, is a form of grace; for failure, as much or more than success, is our schoolmaster. Failure today teaches us how to succeed tomorrow. Today's failure expresses no malediction, no wrathful vengeance, in God; a not unkindly reality teaches us, often through failure, the meaning and value of success—the truth and sanity which make life coherent and whole.

Since no one has all the answers, an individual can hardly be blamed for trying to live by the answers he has inherited. Whether these answers, bequeathed to him by well-meaning but fallible ancestors, are or are not true is the inescapable question. With this question skepticism begins. Yet an individual has only seventy years, more or less, at his disposal. While waiting for careful thinkers to decide what is and what is not true, he still must rise every morning, go to bed every night, and fill the time between as creatively as he can.

Further, the men who devote the whole of adult life to intellectual probing cannot be said to possess all the truth; every man, whether specialist or layman, must live by what he thinks in his heart. In the absence of infallible answers among specialists and laymen alike, there is a provisional but not permanent justification for fundamentalist or pre-skeptical religion. No man can start where he is not; every man must start where he is. A twenty-year-old cannot wait till he is forty to start living. If he receives a set of answers, however unexamined, from his parents and teachers and preachers, there is much to be said for his attempt to live by them—till better ones appear.

The skeptical method itself demands that every alleged answer, not merely those officially approved, be thoroughly investigated. An answer can be sincerely investigated only if it is for a time honestly accepted and put to work. The skeptical method does not begin with rejection, rather with provisional acceptance, with trial, experimentation, and testing. The youth's inherited answers proved in some degree workable and satisfying for his parents. Our fathers and mothers have fed and clothed and sheltered us. We cannot feel that everything they have taught us is false. The possibility of growth rises precisely at this point. In accepting and testing inherited conclusions, a youth sooner or later discovers their apparent inadequacy—from his own point of view. For a time he may discard his parents' conclusions altogether, when, to his surprise, he discovers truth not included in them or fails to see in them the truth his parents saw.

At this point the weakness of pre-skeptical irreligion appears; in throwing away parental conclusions, lock, stock, and barrel, the hasty youth casts away the true with the false. To work out, with trial and error, his own set of answers, he feels that he must begin from scratch. He becomes a self-conscious skeptic; in fact he is seeking a more inclusive religion than the one taught him in childhood. Later he may discover, to his surprise and not a little to his chagrin, that some truth was present in his parents' answers; this he will then fit, with new meaning, into his own understanding. But he did no wrong, at the beginning, to accept his parents' system of answers as a working hypothesis. Only by accepting and testing them could their adequacy or inadequacy appear to him. Since reality is seldom if ever in perfect harmony with any system of ideas, there is much to be said for a youth's acceptance of the system someone—a parent, teacher, or preacher—has found workable. Truth, in our limited grasp, possesses both the greatness and finitude of logic. Truth, as we view it, is always a proposition or series of propositions, a formula or series of formulae; our logic is always a straight line, while our life is always a curve. The straight line of logic and the curve of life never exactly coincide. God is greater than either our logic or our life, for he includes both in one purpose, one world, one pedagogy; the difference between logic and life makes our learning possible. Inadequate logic puts a strait jacket on life, but life eventually breaks through—at the demand of God. While waiting for a view of God with room for logic as well as life, the youth must live, and be as logical as he can. At twenty he cannot live with the more inclusive view of seventy. He is therefore not unwise to begin at twenty with the best logic he has received, with the most inclusive view he has found.

Pre-skeptical faith becomes unjustifiable the moment our twenty-year-old discovers truths he cannot harmonize with received answers. As a rule, the twenty-year-old will not depart from received answers without great provocation. He will manage somehow to hold himself and the received answers together, for sanity requires a measure of continuity. A professor once put it this way: "Don't let go with your hands till you find something firm for your feet." Sanity demands that a youth proceed the same way in religion. When he finds discrepancies in the faith that is old to him, he will put it down, as long as possible, to his lack of understanding. He will say to himself: "Life and logic do not fit; I will therefore put life in one pocket and logic in another, and wait for better light."

But the youth may experience increasingly, and painfully, the discrepancy between received answers and reality. Pre-skeptical faith becomes bomb-shelter faith when the twenty-year-old, faced with real challenge, says to himself: "I refuse to consider the fact of discrepancy." Pre-skeptical faith thus becomes retreat from God, retreat from logic, retreat from life. At this point the youth prefers safety to truth. He may in time prefer unreality to reality, and enter the world of dreams. He may become a sentimentalist, an emotionalist, an aesthete—in desperate escape from the challenge God presents to his system of ideas. He hides from the process server, evades the subpoena of reality. He withdraws into the bomb shelter and hopes devoutly the storm will blow itself out. But a sense of responsibility, the nature and demand of God, follows him into the bomb shelter and points a long finger. He must obey the call or remain a fugitive forever. The bomb shelter was built with haste, with sticks and stones of protective rationalizations; the storm may destroy it. He may create a set of fictitious definitions to keep his peace of mind. He may attempt the intellectual dodge. So great is the power of the intellect that it has built many a durable bomb shelter. The shelter will sustain every emergency except a direct hit. Many an adult has lived from twenty to seventy safely hidden from God's call to growth. He has turned his mind to money-making or to some mechanical or professional trick; he has striven with enthusiasm to forget the inner summons to creative struggle. He has walked into maturity a mechanic or a professor, but no longer a man. Inner peace, the peace of the bomb shelter, has been purchased at too great a price—the price of integrity, the price of essential manhood. He may shout down his inner disquiet by singing hymns or "Internationales," but the clamor never wholly extinguishes the disturbing whisper within. Should he succeed altogether in silencing the inner whisper, he may gain the world, but he has lost his soul.

Five Varieties of Religious Inadequacy

When a youth makes up his mind to look squarely and honestly at his religious inheritance, he discovers at least five areas of inadequacy. These caricatures of true religion drive him toward a temporary or prolonged break with religion itself; they are therefore worthy of thoughtful, if brief, examination. Each man experiences these forms of religious inadequacy in a different sequence; I list them here as I experienced them.

The first caricature of true religion closes its eyes to the actual problems of this world, and opens them only upon *the world above*. On this view, life's serious business is escape from the wheel of existence, preoccupation with immortality, the struggle to enter heaven; the earth and its life have no value of their own. To take this view seriously is to abandon the heroic attempt to make the more and the better replace the less and the worse—in politics, economics, race relations, morality, and even in religion. A deep unwillingness to share the struggle, an enervating cowardice, a lethal lethargy, play tricks on the mind. God is relegated to a dimension above and out of touch with the world. This view is sufficiently widespread to constitute a real barrier to the growth of religion itself; its presence in our churches is a comfort to the old and the weak, but makes the churches' message seem irrelevant to every this-worldly task.

Where the first caricature of true religion seeks its fulfillment above the world, the second seeks fulfillment *beyond the end of the world*. The all-absorbing focus of attention is the Second Coming of Christ, the Last Judgment, the Battle of Armageddon. An attempt is made to put the Revelation of St. John on a time schedule. The Apocalypse predicts God's final victory *for* man beyond tragedy, but literal interpretation sees only the judgment of this world, not its creation or completion. Judgment is a stage in creation; crisis is a stage in process. God's energy thrusts us forward from behind, while God's purpose draws us onward from ahead. The second caricature, however, divorces judgment from creation. On its view, judgment ends this world; redemption begins another after this one is destroyed. The interplay of judgment and redemption in this world is not perceived at all. A youth, confronted with this caricature of religion, may feel that religion itself is irrelevant to the present world dilemma.

The third variety of inadequate religion is the view that *the church exists for its own sake,* not for the sake of the world. According to this view, God's presence and power are in this world, but only in and for the church—sometimes understood as *my* church. The sanctity of *my* church may be founded upon the apostolic succession, or the literal Bible, or right doctrine, or baptism by immersion, or papal infallibility, or prohibition. The sect-centered disciple thinks primarily of his own company of "the elect." When he thinks of the total Church—the fellowship of all who seek and serve God—he may exclude from his thought the world outside the Church. God, to whom the Church bears witness, is regarded as the private possession of the Church; God has no interest in the world outside the Church, in the dwelling place of the damned. The whole family of man, the human race, is excluded automatically from the divine concern. The love of God wears a private label; it is the monopoly of the "redeemed." "God so loved *the world*"; "God sent not his

Son into *the world* to condemn the world; but that *the world* through him might be saved" (John 3:16, 17)—these words are forgotten or "safely" interpreted.

The arms of God embrace all men—worldlings and churchlings alike. God summons all men to a better approximation of his will. Neither worldling nor churchling privately possesses his love. The churchling, in prayer and praise, is or ought to be alert to the divine summons as the worldling is not; in race relations and common justice it is sometimes the other way around. Insofar as the churchling confines the love of God to the apostolic succession, to papal infallibility, to right doctrine, to baptism by immersion, or to prohibition, he may convert the weak to his fold, but the strong he converts to worldliness. It is the world which God is creating in his image, not a sect, or even the fellowship of sects. The church, when it is faithful, is a *means,* not the *end,* of grace.

The fourth caricature which converts young men to irreligion is *biblical literalism.* The claim of absolute biblical infallibility is inviting to a few but unacceptable to many. God is more than the private possession of the Old and New Testaments. The writings of other religions also bear witness to him. The writings of the saints and martyrs within Christian history add their testimony to the greatness and goodness of God. The Bible, which records the dealings of God with Israel and first-century Christians, is an inspiration to faith, not faith's final test. The call of God comes to us in and through the Bible, the call to responsible love, the call to the better and the more.

It is obvious that the Bible cannot speak to men who do not take it seriously. It is equally obvious that to substitute the Bible for the God to whom it witnesses is to commit idolatry. Not the Bible, but God, sustains and creates the world. The Bible, designed as a channel of revelation, becomes the whole of revelation—and forward movement is ended. The channel becomes an obstacle. One should not worship a telescope, but look through it at the stars. One should not worship a microscope, but look through it at worlds in miniature. The purpose of the Bible is not to imprison but to release faith; it is not an end but a means. "The Lord hath yet more light and truth to break forth from his word." To consider the Bible as the whole of God's self-revelation is to drive honest minds away from religion.

The fifth caricature is *self-centered religion*. To be sure, we are—individually—objects of divine concern. Our personal struggle to find the way is important. Our predicament in life and logic is unique. Nevertheless, our actual dignity as children of God is quickly distorted into egoism. The trouble with self-centered religion is not its *in*iquity, but its *un*iquity. Outside the egoist's circle of concern is the world of second-class men. Self-centered religion is the sorrow of every social effort to create freedom and faithfulness in fellowship. In the struggle of man to know the truth, the religious egoist appoints himself a pope, considers his own findings final and the wisdom of other men a form of folly. In economics, the religious egoist thinks of himself as "self-made"; he glories in rugged individualism, considers "Communist" every whole-family effort of the human race to meet its needs. The religious egoist's own struggle is dramatic; other people's struggles are tiresome. Remember the self-display, the exhibitionism, of the old-fashioned "testimony meeting." Across nationalist barriers the religious egoist walks a lonely road; he regards men of other nations as "beyond the pale": this is called "insular thinking" in England, "isolationism" in America.

One must begin where he is and with whatever answers he has found, yet these caricatures of true religion make a measure of irreligion inevitable.

Inverted Dogmatism

A great gulf is fixed between true skepticism, which seeks endlessly to separate the unreal from the real, and "closed" irreligion, which is in fact an inverted dogmatism, a negative finalism, a rejecting infallibility. The position is understandable and not without integrity, yet its assumption of finality makes it another premature maturity. Every man who has been forced to surrender the received answers of adolescence, whether liberal or conservative, has dwelt awhile, and not without creativity, in this vale of sorrow. Pre-skeptical irreligion is the view that no objective reality supports truth and sanity, that the call of man to growth in love is a fiction of his own imagination. If nothing can be known as objectively true, irreligion cannot be known. If no objective reality supports man's search for the real, skepticism itself has no further work to do. If no reality exists, the effort to cast away unreality is heroic nonsense. Only a man who believes strongly can be a skeptic; only he can be interested in preserving the true from corruption and distortion. It is accurate, therefore, to say that if pre-skeptical irreligion is final for man, skepticism is ended. Skepticism itself forces open the narrow confines of pre-skeptical irreligion; man's concern for truth and sanity thrusts him beyond the premature conclusion that truth and sanity are illusions. The attempt to understand the nature and demand of reality is not a luxury but a necessity.

The Honest Attempt to See

A normal youth is endowed not only with a capacity for faithfulness to the views of the persons he loves, and who love him, but also with native curiosity. Not that he loves his parents less, but that he loves the truth more. Not that he holds the received opinions in contempt, but that he can never feel satisfied with them till he has examined the alternatives. He does not know, from first-hand experience, what is on the other side of the fixed boundaries of his parents' world. He has been brought up on one side of the tracks, intellectually, morally, and religiously; God has filled him with a keen if not wholly conscious desire to know the nature of the forbidden. Curiosity is not evil, but good. Were it not for the constant probing of curiosity, mankind would still worship gods of wood and stone, would still practice slavery, would still leave girl babies to die on the hillside. God has placed in every man a holy itch to move beyond the sacrosanct to the unexplored. As long as man is man, he will desire to know what is behind the locked doors of life and thought.

The itch to know what is unknown or condemned drives youth from passive acceptance of parental opinion—in politics no less than religion—first to doubt parental infallibility, and then perhaps to cast away, in the heat of revolt, the good along with the evil. It is easier to buy or sell a mountain than to pan for gold in the clay. It is harder to separate wheat from chaff than to eat bread made from both. Skepticism is hard work; we are not by nature enthusiastic for toil, especially without tangible reward. More often than not we become irreligious only when driven to do so by logic or life—against our resistance to change, our native inertia. One does not easily switch from pre-skeptical religion to pre-skeptical irreligion; the change does not come painlessly or cheaply. But once the change is made, coerced by life's imponderable logic, the expended energy cannot be quickly regained. It takes a youth many years to accumulate enough energy of mind and spirit to throw off what he considers a burden; he cannot overnight find sufficient energy for a second, and closer, grapple with God. In five or ten years energy in thought and life will again reach creative pitch; then only, after the interval of rest, will our youth move forward. Rest, as well as conflict, is necessary for growth—even the premature rest of pre-skeptical irreligion. A youth may also move from pre-skeptical irreligion to pre-skeptical religion—for the same reasons. He may revolt against his parents' liberal finalism; curiosity may drive him to investigate another "view" than the one he has received.

A youth cannot move forward from pre-skeptical irreligion till he perceives with clarity and conviction that thinking is one thing, a final conclusion is another, though the two are closely related. When skepticism is a question, it inevitably cracks open skepticism as the final answer. Only one conclusion can sustain skeptical questioning: the view that God questions all human conclusions. When skepticism is fully alert to separate the false from the true, it is also fully aware that truth is necessary to man. Pre-skeptical irreligion is skepticism as conclusion, the end of skepticism as question. Irreligion as final conclusion, the halfway house of marching youth, asserts that nothing but energy is real; skepticism as method, a wholly different thing, seeks the purpose as well as the fact of energy—at any cost. The "matter only" skeptic accepts the dogma that nothing but energy is real; he is no longer a skeptic in method, for the skeptic in method seeks to distinguish creative from uncreative uses of energy. To the "matter only" skeptic, "creative" and "uncreative" are value or purpose concepts, and as such without root in reality; for him, only energy, itself indefinable, is real; purpose is illusion. Skepticism as method will in time burst open the premature dogma of purposeless energy. Skepticism as method will always, in the logic of life, crack open the closed infallibility of the pre-skeptical. If no purpose exists, what is the purpose of the skeptic?

In point of fact, pre-skeptical irreligion seldom if ever accepts unconditionally the dogma that nothing but energy is real. As James Luther Adams has understood, men never stop being religious; they only change their religion. Men do not cancel their belief in purpose; they only alter their understanding of its content. What usually happens is this: a youth is given a set of answers, together with the claim that the answers are complete. He then discovers, slowly and painfully but surely, that the received answers are not complete, that there are many things in the universe not covered by the formula. If his parents are fundamentalists, in fact whether or not in name, they have taught him in the main that only heaven is real, that the earth will pass away like any illusion. A normally healthy youth finds that his earthly desires are remarkably strong illusions; indeed his parents and teachers, in point of practice, consider such earthly realities as money, clothing, and professional advancement matters of concern and anguish. The youth suspects that something is wrong with the formula, that the earth and its energies are more important than his parents have taught him. With anguish of soul he may reach the conviction that the earth is real and heaven an illusion. He will not be wholly wrong; he will be wholly right in his realization that God is fully involved in the here and the now. In Christian theology, our youth has discovered the world which God creates and sustains—neglected altogether in logic, though not altogether in life, by his parents. Christians have always taught, though they have sometimes forgotten, that the total actual energy of the world is the impersonal or neutral or preparatory presence of God. To believe in "energy only" is therefore to be a demi-theist, a believer in half of God.

Christians, oddly enough, have often written "Forbidden" on the door of the world. The youth who tears off the label and opens the door is normal; moreover, he is doing the neglected work of God. He is restoring the other half of Christian truth—this world and its full importance as the theater of divine operations. So world-shaking is a youth's discovery of God's world that he finds himself for a time incapable of thinking of God. He can think of energy but not purpose. Years later, when he is more than an amateur skeptic, he will discover that reality is not only a quantity but also a quality, not only energy but purpose, not only what he sees with his eyes but also what he does not see with his eyes—responsibility, mutuality, brotherhood, an irresistible call which echoes in the whole life of man.

A long and difficult pilgrimage is not unusual. At each stage one sees as much as he can from where he stands. First, he sees what his parents see; he looks at life through their spectacles, and only at that part of life which parental censorship permits. Second, he takes off the spectacles and has a look around, beyond the approved area of investigation; he sets forth to learn what he can for himself. God is irresistible; he demands that a youth make the great adventure on his own. For a time the youth is so enamored of what he sees, precisely because he sees it with his own eyes, that he discards what others—particularly his parents—have seen. He rejects one half-truth, and promptly substitutes another. He accepts the world as it is, but rejects the demand of God which is other than and better than present worldly achievement. If the youth accepts the world as it is and rejects the world as it ought to be, he settles down into a new infallibility called realism, a new denial of the call to growth, a new unforgivable sin; for the rigor of the summons to mutuality he substitutes *rigor mortis*. Life is so constructed, however, that a youth, though determined upon an exclusive commitment to the here and the now, is soon forced to the discovery that much of the here and the now is neither true nor sane, that "what now is" is summoned everlastingly to become "what ought to be"—that even in the here and the now it is reality which sustains the unreal, not the unreal which sustains reality. The world is a school: God sustains the student, the human race, in the midst of failures; and God summons the student to a truth and a sanity not yet in his possession.

Five Varieties of Irreligious Inadequacy

We have seen five varieties of inadequate religion; five varieties of irreligious inadequacy are equally discernible. The first is *pantheism*—the dogma that God is not more than the world. Pantheism is the positive content of atheism; one is no longer concerned with the far and the beyond, but exclusively with the near and the here. As an atheist for ten years, pantheism, as I have defined it, was the content of my belief. Pantheism takes this world seriously and rejoices in it. Not to love this world is to forsake God, who made the world, saw that it was good, and loved it; who so loved this world that he gave himself in the flesh of Jesus, and the flesh of the saints, to complete its half-finished creation. We may or may not have another home in a beautiful Isle of Somewhere; we do have approximately a seventy-year lease as individuals, and perhaps a seventy-million year lease as a family, on this planet, this floating Isle, spinning and speeding in space. If this planet exhausts its usefulness, there are others which may be, or may be made to be, serviceable. On any terms, our clear duty is to make the most of our present privilege. Let us not feel ourselves strangers in any part of God's world or to any of our fellow pilgrims. We ought to feel "at home" on this planet, if only for the reason that God has placed us here. The pantheist inadequacy is this: "what ought to be" is cancelled; by definition "what is" is all. Growth occurs among pantheists as among other folk, for God and his demand surround and summon us all, but in pantheist logic growth is fiction; change is fact. "What now is" is final. The summons to the more and the better, and the power to become the sons of God, are denied. If there is nothing more than what presently exists, the unattained is illusion. All that is left is the endless monotony of change; there is neither up nor down, progress nor retrogression—only the buzzing of chimera in the void. The sense of meaninglessness drives the honest pilgrim beyond irreligion.

Religious humanism perceives that man is over nature under God; however, *irreligious humanism,* the first cousin of pantheism, asserts that man is nature's child, and nature's plaything. He may in some sense fashion nature to his will, but his will and his body are nature's vassals. God, who has driven and drawn the evolutionary process to richness, variety, and consciousness, is outside the narrow circle of concern. The irreligious humanist is a bootstrap theologian. If he believes that universal brotherhood is inevitable, he is no longer irreligious, for he considers "what ought to be" more powerful than "what now is." If a man who considers himself the fatherless child of nature believes that universal brotherhood is inevitable, he is guilty of wishful thinking. The nature we have known is red in tooth and claw; war rather than peace is its character. The wish for universal brotherhood is the father of the thought; fulfillment has no root in reality. However, the very wish for fulfillment, for brotherhood, bears witness to the nature and demand of God. *The irreligious humanist must choose: either reality does, or does not, correspond to man's desire for brotherhood.* Man as he is, is more often uncreative than creative; universal brotherhood is achievable only if man is sustained, corrected, and directed by a reality which transcends him.

A third garden variety of irreligious inadequacy is *secularism*—the view that reality does not include religion. To be sure, skepticism must endlessly separate meaningful and moral religion from sanctified caste systems, glorified political empires, petrified institutions, and frozen infallibilities. False religion must be separated from the true, because true religion is basic to man. Man is going to be religious whether or no; he is going to be a committed, devoted enthusiast of the *status quo,* if not of the better and the more. The skeptic's business is to separate the worship of the *status quo* from true religion, that man may live and grow in and toward the real.

Secularism performs a necessary service when it rejects the merely backward look of pseudo religion and begins to look ahead. Secularism is man's ally and friend when it rejects the merely upward look of exclusive otherworldliness and insists that this world is our assignment. Secularism is a human necessity when it rejects the minority view that the church exists for its own sake alone, and labors to enclose the whole wide world within the circle of sanity. Secularism is a divine requirement when it rejects the view that truth exists solely in the Bible, and seeks for all men the truth that makes men free and freedom meaningful.

Secularism is the friend of freedom when it defends freedom against political and religious tyrannies. Secularism becomes the enemy of freedom when it becomes the dogmatism of a Hitler or a Stalin; doctrinaire secularism empties the world of the absolute demand for responsibility, mutuality, or love. When secularism substitutes the tyranny of race or class or nationality—specially in the name of religion—for the summons to freedom and faithfulness in fellowship, it is a final and deadly betrayal of freedom. The spiritual emptiness of secularism drives men beyond irreligion.

A fourth irreligious inadequacy is *scientism*. Scientism is the pseudo religion, the romanticism, of the irreligious; it glorifies the present achievements of science and ignores the surrounding reality which summons science every day to new work and new venture. Few scientists are disciples of scientism, for a scientist is a practicing skeptic—alert to separate fact from fiction. Scientism has one value: many achievements of science are indeed commendable; even football teams are entitled to cheerleaders. The failure to recognize moral as well as neutral reality makes scientism amoral. Scientism is another theology of the bootstraps, another form of self-sufficiency, for one reason: it does not see that reality is the parent, not the child, of science. The view that God demands more than present achievement keeps both scientist and saint at work: for man's requirements are moral as well as mechanical. It is theoretically possible that modern man may be forced to make a final choice between the bomb offered by the scientist and the brotherhood offered by the saint. On any terms, the first is the spur to the second. Since man cannot live by mechanism alone, he finds himself thrust beyond irreligion.

The fifth irreligious inadequacy is *Communism.* It claims infallibility in its understanding of truth: it rejects martyrs and saints from its register of workers; it denies the reality that summons present freedom and dignity to greater freedom and faithfulness. Communism reduces the individual to statistical importance, denies the depth relation between the individual and God, claims finality for secular tyranny. Neither freedom nor faithfulness makes headway when dominion over the minds of men is exercised by a Russian dictator and Politburo. The threat of the Communist lock step drives man beyond irreligion.

Pre-skeptical irreligion is a detour, not a highway. Living commitment to the God who unites energy and purpose makes faith skeptical and skepticism faithful. The mature and growing Christian is neither more nor less than one who sees that truth and sanity are the structure of the universe, the nature and demand of God; that the summons to responsible love, to whole-family mutuality, was made flesh in Jesus, shed abroad in the saints, and is now the inevitable, yet resistible, option of all institutions and men. At every moment God offers us an alternative to futility.

Inadequacy, whether religious or irreligious, is not enough for man. Further, it is not necessary, for God has equipped us with courage. Cowardice or miscarriage in any form need not detain us. God endlessly increases his own kind of life, responsibility or love, in the civilization and the soul that are open to him. In his faithfulness is our security; in his demand is our summons to growth toward the full stature of Christ; in his gift is our power to become his sons.

Faith: At War with Skepticism

GOD CONFRONTS US in the world and in the soul. When we insist that God confronts us only in the soul, men who discover the reality of the world are bound, for a time, to become atheists. But if atheism is a natural reaction to inadequate religion, the move beyond atheism is a natural reaction to the inadequacy of atheism—to men who discover the reality of the soul. The discovery of spiritual or moral reality makes a man again a theist. However, in the first flush of the move beyond atheism, a man may lose his hard-won sense of the reality of the world, in which God also confronts him; he becomes short-tempered with atheism, and even more with atheists. He has discovered and accepted the reality of the soul, but rejected the reality of the world. One half of adequate religion is at war with the other half. No peace worth having can be won until a man perceives that in the world as well as in the soul one God confronts him.

Beyond Atheism

Many influences drove me forward from pre-skeptical irreligion to post-skeptical faith. The skepticism I had developed, had developed me; it was strong, but insufficiently established. Its true value was not seen with clarity. It had

become to me a final view of the world; as such, its usefulness as a method of understanding the world was ended.
It was positive enough as a belief, but only in purposeless
energy. Most simply, my skepticism was insufficiently
skeptical. Skepticism is the necessary endeavor to distinguish sense from nonsense. To me, in its first flush of
power, skepticism was simple reductionism—the attempt
to reduce everything to nothing, to explain the more by
the less. Reductionism performs an essential service; it
clears away debris, removes the false to make room for the
true. But reductionism alone is a denial of skepticism, for
skepticism, by nature, is also constructionism—the attempt
to make the good prevail; it seeks the better and the more
to replace the worse and the less. It seeks, not the absence,
but the presence, of the adequate.

During the ten years that I was an atheist, convinced
that nothing on earth or in heaven could alter my opinion,
I had tested my negative faith in every dimension of
thought and life—so far as my mind could reach. I had
fashioned a dogmatic conclusion, a total denial of meaning in the world. But the Sahara Desert, which was my
view of reality, seemed less and less attractive as a dwelling place. I had reduced everything to nothing in my
mind, and was left with nothing in my hands and in my
heart. Selfishness was released from all bonds, but selfishness in Sahara provides little rejoicing. I had isolated myself from all men in my haste to draw near to them. Whatever I believed, most men still believed in a moral and
meaningful world, and in some measure accepted their
responsibility to and for the common good. Most men believed—naively I thought—in personal responsibility, and
thus constituted a community—a fellowship of commitment, something more than a spatial collection of selves.
Atheism meant to me that I was no longer part of a responsible universe; responsibility, in any form, was no
longer required of me by the nature of reality. I had there-

fore cut myself adrift from humankind. I had fought for and achieved freedom from religion, freedom from spiritual and ethical responsibility and demand. The freedom was fine, but I had not counted on the increasing loneliness. I was something other than a responsible member of the human race. I had walked away from the bondage of the human community into glorious liberty, only to find myself a solitary exile on the outer rim of the world.

I would never have emerged from pre-skeptical irreligion without endless help—from persons too numerous to mention and influences too complex to define. Two factors above others drove me to theistic faith. One, as I have suggested, was my lonely isolation from the common commitment to responsibility, morality, and community. No one could trust me—neither my father, nor my wife, nor my children, nor my employer. I could not trust myself. Miserable with such an existence, I developed an almighty longing to become again a member of the human community. I wanted to become the kind of man in whom other men could put a measure of confidence. At the bottom of the Depression, during eight months of unemployment, I was forced to swallow male pride and live on my wife's earnings as a schoolteacher. Presently a new job was offered me—quite unaccountably and generously. It looked very much as if it might be the last. I grasped it, as a drowning man grasps at a straw, and it held. I determined to give the new job my honest effort, my sincere best. For five years I had not believed in personal responsibility, a thing called faithfulness. Faithfulness is a moral principle; from my standpoint moral principles were simon-pure fictions. In the effort to be logical I had cast away the "notion" that reality required me to do my best. I had often said to myself: "I am under no obligation to give an honest day's work for an honest day's pay." The idea of obligation was developed by employers to make employees put their backs into it. Keep up appearances—yes. This, one must do.

When the new job was offered and I had accepted it, a turning point was reached in my experience. Religion, so far as I was concerned, had nothing to do with it. Not for five more years did I believe in God as Reality—the energy of the world and the purpose of the energy. I knew, economically speaking, that my fortunes had grown steadily worse since I had become an atheist. "Forces in existence" —beyond my control—had driven me into a corner. I could work, with honest heart and mind, or starve. And I preferred to work. I went to the new job with conscious dedication—not to God, as yet unknown to me, but to myself and the people who had called me to serve them. I resolved to put all beliefs in my side pocket and give my honest best to the task at hand.

Undoubtedly this experience was the beginning of personal responsibility or morality, and therefore the beginning of religion. For religion, whatever else it may be, is personal commitment to responsibility—for oneself and for all men. Religion becomes theist when it perceives that this responsibility, for all men and for all things, is the nature and demand of God. But religion, though less than theist, is still good religion when it accepts responsibility— whether or not it is aware that responsibility is the structure of the real.

Precisely speaking, I was a religious atheist—for five more years. I was an atheist in creed, in theology, in dogma, but personally committed to responsibility for my family, for my job, for myself. Creed, theology, and dogma were still to be converted, and this was the more troublesome task. On the one hand I was committed to responsibility; on the other I did not believe that reality is responsible. Nor could I find any sort of loophole in my systematic atheism. Responsibility to me was, and is, another word for love. I had accepted responsibility for the first time in many years, and I found myself in better harmony not only with others but also with myself. I had therefore accepted love as a personal obligation, yet remained convinced that reality is totally indifferent to love—being then unable to distinguish between energy, which is indifferent to love, and the purpose of energy, which is not. Love, as I had found in practice, was a good idea, but neither more nor less than a personal whim; it suited me; it was not the structure and demand of the universe.

Through three years of graduate study, required by my profession, I remained an unreconstructed atheist—the more easily so because the ideas presented by all but one of my teachers formed the sterile fundamentalism I had long discarded, and to which, in the nature of things, I could never return. After graduate school were four additional years of postgraduate study, and two in preparing a thesis, before I received the Ph.D. My postgraduate professors were not afraid of skepticism; they had learned that skepticism is an indispensable part of human reason, lest the unreal be accepted with the real—and the last state of man be worse than the first. These men were amused rather than alarmed when I expressed my atheist convictions; to my surprise they did not throw me down the front steps of the Temple. I did not believe that friendship, another word for responsibility or love, is structural to reality, yet I had found needed friends. I could speak freely for the first time in many years. My ideas were not at once dismissed as irrelevant or damned as irreverent.

Nonetheless, for two more years I remained an atheist. During this period I was forced by the curriculum to read the major classics I had hitherto avoided. A great choir of voices from across the centuries—Plato, Augustine, St. Francis, Aquinas, Dante, Pascal (to mention but a few)— spoke to my condition from profound wrestling with life. I fell in love with these voices, though I could not then accept their testimony that the universe is responsible. The universe, I continued to believe, was not irresponsible; it was simply nonresponsible. Responsibility was an idea invented by men to aid their survival; it was not a true idea, not the structure of reality.

Early in my third year of postgraduate study I said one day to my wife: "It's a strange thing: I am still a convinced atheist, yet aware that I stand in the presence of God." A tree of faith in positive reality was growing through the concrete of "closed" negation. About this time I gave three addresses which accurately represented the state of my thoughts. In one I described a Christian atheist—a man who believed not at all in God, Christ, Holy Spirit, the soul, immortality, the atonement, the resurrection, present providence or final victory; this man, however, believed that the self-giving of Jesus to and for the world was, and is, the solid foundation of mental health. He therefore dedicated himself to self-giving, that love might grow in the homes and hearts of men. In my definition, this man was both an atheist and a Christian. Except that the standard churches might not receive him, there was nothing to prevent his active membership in a Christian fellowship. The other addresses developed the following themes: "Whether there is any God or not, Jesus was his Son"; and a week later, "Whether there is any God or not, he has played the largest role in history."

About this time I accepted the invitation of an atheist friend, Joseph Wheless, to public debate at Rosoff's Restaurant on Forty-third Street in Manhattan. Our question was already selected: "Has religion benefited mankind?" He defined religion as otherworldly superstition and nonsense, mankind's greatest curse. I defined religion as acceptance of responsibility for oneself and one's neighbors around the world, mankind's greatest asset. Both definitions are true—in part. Religion as blind obedience to Roman ecclesiasticism, or to fundamentalist biblicism, has undoubtedly burdened man, though it has also given him

strength to bear the burden, and a deep sense of personal
if not social responsibility; St. Francis of Assisi, whom all
men love, who loved all men, was both a Roman Catholic
and a biblical literalist.

To shorten a long story, I developed, very slowly, a
wholesale commitment to the Christian faith—as distinct
from fundamentalism, Romanism, and Culture-Protestant-
ism. To my mind, the Christian faith, stripped of secondary elements, was best expressed in the classical creeds and
the great writings of the fathers. I cast away skepticism
itself, except as a protection against pietism, quietism, and
escape. I became, in thought and in word, increasingly
and prematurely post-skeptical. Skepticism, I believed, had
accomplished its purpose: it had destroyed superstition
and literalism; it had widened my acquaintance with reality; it had helped me to find a bigger God; it had led
me to the conviction that responsibility or love is the nature and demand of the universe. I now believed that responsibility or love was made flesh in Jesus, and shed
abroad in the world through the Church. With sincere
blindness I considered faith at war with skepticism, and
the task of every Christian to uproot skepticism altogether
—in himself and all men. For a time I thought of becoming
a Roman Catholic.

Overconversion is as dangerous as underconversion. I
made the common orthodox mistake of considering skepticism, which is faith's necessary ally, as faith's deadliest
enemy. I cultivated the gothic mind—its upward look toward God, its backward look toward the saints, its inward
look of self-examination and prayer. Neither the outward
look nor the forward look held any interest for me. The
outward look was superficial sociology, the forward look
utopianism.

I was fully committed to the Christian faith, but in
frozen and otherworldly form. Man's business, as I understood it, was to seek the eternal and forsake the temporal.

I appointed myself the foe of skepticism; rational integrity was the self-sufficient pride of the mind; every effort of man to solve his problems in this world was the self-sufficient pride of the will. Human reason and human strength were either destructive or futile. The eternal was all, the temporal nothing.

Faith Is Reasonable

The one God who confronts us in the world and in the soul will not leave us content with half of adequate religion. It is he who thrusts us beyond our schizophrenic split between the world without the soul and the soul without the world. As Von Huegel put it, our task, the task of God, is to spiritualize civilization and to civilize spirituality. Both the world and the soul belong to God; both reason and revelation are his.

It is commonly understood that reason must endeavor to separate fact from fiction; this is the skeptic's obvious and essential task. It is less commonly appreciated that integrity of reason demands commitment to what is found to be true. Until a man is committed to the truth he sees, whether in science or religion, he has no basis for the judgment that so-called truth is error. A third element is necessary also: the patient realization that what one thinks is true and what is true are not identical. The fourth element, psychologically speaking, may be most necessary of all: the strengthening realization that God, or Reality, actually participates, in some degree, in the truth one has struggled to see. This realization is the basis of sanity and joy; it is called "practical certainty"—pending later and better information; it is the point at which thought becomes action. The fifth element is the foundation of the other four. In importance it is actually first; in personal experience it often comes last. It is the clear consciousness that God is actually there, awaiting discovery—that he is not *against* man but *for* man, since it is he who sustains man. Further, he is not a passive onlooker but an active ally; further still, he confronts nations and men with the terrible choice of creative co-operation or extinction; and finally, he has sufficient power to sustain our freedom yet correct its perversion—to overcome our evil with good. One might call these elements: skepticism, commitment, humility (the possibility of growth), practical certainty or action, and confidence or hope. Christians will recognize them in personal experience as (1) seeking the way, (2) decision or discipleship, (3) repentance or self-examination, (4) living by faith (justification), and (5) the realization that one is fully grasped by sufficient grace (regeneration).

Confusion enters reason from the popular misconception that reason and faith are at war. Reason is falsely alleged to be only the separation of fact from fiction. But unless reason holds fast what it sees to be true, it has no basis of measuring or separating what is false. Unless reason recognizes its fallibility, it has no room for growth. Unless reason is convinced that reality participates in its conclusions, it has no basis of action. Unless reason believes that reality is there, awaiting discovery, there is no point in reason's painful search. *Faith is intrinsic or structural to reason itself.* Reason can accept only what it sees to be true. Precisely this acceptance, this commitment, is what is meant by faith. As C. S. Lewis has understood, faith is the art of holding on to what one's reason has told him is true. Because faith is loyalty to what one regards as true, it is not an enterprise separate from reason but an essential reasonable activity. Humility, the possibility of growth, is likewise essential to reason, for, on any terms, reason becomes irrational when it assumes finality or infallibility for its conclusions.

Five elements, then, are central to the reasoning process: the sifting of the false from the true, firm loyalty to what is seen to be true, honest recognition that the truth and one's understanding of it are not identical, practical certainty that reality actually participates in one's conclusions, and confidence in the sustaining adequacy of the real.

But the question is also central: In what way are the five elements related? They are not a mere series; they dynamically interpenetrate and are mutually strengthening.

When one stops to think about it, it seems obvious enough that the five elements—skepticism, commitment, humility, practical certainty, and confidence—must be presented in reverse order if their relative importance is to be understood. Every man must begin where he is, to be sure; yet both psychologically and factually, confidence in the existence and adequacy of God is the foundation of the other four. Confidence that God is prior to our discovery is the strength of our search. Skepticism cannot separate reality from unreality unless convinced that reality exists to be separated. Skepticism cannot cleanse fiction from fact unless convinced that fact is prior to fiction and that it is able to survive the cleansing.

Skepticism cannot stand alone. It is itself the requirement of faith and humility: faith that reality waits to be known, and humility that one's present grasp of it is insufficient. Faith therefore involves not only *firm commitment* to what is regarded as true, but also the *firm conviction* that reality is there, awaiting man's clearer understanding. If reality is there, awaiting discovery, it is clearly prior to the search for it; indeed it is reality or God who has driven man to the search, sustains him while he seeks, participates in some degree in the truth that he sees, and waits with joy and gladness at the end of the seeking.

Our clearer understanding of God is dependent upon skepticism, fully mature and fully active, yet God does not depend upon skepticism; skepticism depends upon God. Further, our growing grasp of God's nature and demand, always conditioned, always fallible, is dependent upon careful skeptical work, yet skepticism itself is dependent upon the faith with which we begin. We can declare nothing to be false unless we have made up our minds that something is true. The order of importance and dependence is therefore as follows: truth is prior to and the author of our understanding; it participates in our conclusions; it is greater than our grasp; it demands our firm commitment to the fragment that we see; it requires us to be alert and active in every dimension of our existence, lest error imprison and cripple the life and spirit of man.

The recognition that God is prior to and greater than our grasp of him is the first half of faith; our commitment to his will as we see it is the second half. All religion participates in the second; some religion both participates in the second and perceives the first. This has been called, and is, "the Protestant principle," the oft-neglected genius of Protestantism. The humdrum but essential activity of "proving all things" is the role of skepticism in the service of God.

God does not proceed from faith, but faith from God. Neither God nor faith proceeds from skepticism, but skepticism from both. While faith does not proceed from skepticism, the purging of faith and the growth of faith toward a closer approximation of reality proceed from the work of skepticism—at the demand of God.

The Common Method of Science and Religion

Culturally speaking, it is obvious that religion concerns itself with churches, doctrines, rituals, and charity, while science concerns itself with laboratories, formulae, procedures, and industry. But when you ask what the method of science is, and what the method of religion is, you come not to two answers but to one. The method of religion, as we have seen, includes the belief that there is a reality to be known, firm commitment to the fragment of reality one has found to be true, and the endless endeavor to separate what is true from what is false. The same elements form the method of science: the conviction that there is a reality to be analyzed, firm commitment to the fragment of reality able to survive investigation, and constant effort to drain off the unreal from the real.

One method characterizes science and religion. It is less often realized that one conclusion about the nature and demand of reality likewise characterizes both activities: the conviction that rationality or coherence is the structure of the real. Both science and religion begin with the conviction that reality, which is rational, is prior to the search for it and precedes human understanding.

The New Testament Insists on Skepticism

The Apostle Paul laid down a dual doctrine as central to man's growth in the grace of God. When the King James translation of the Bible was published, the word "prove" meant "test." Note Paul's words: "Prove [test] all things; hold fast that which is good" (I Thessalonians 5:21). It was assumed by Paul, as it is assumed by science and religion, that reality is prior to man's search and greater than man's grasp, that reality sustains man in his search, that reality shines through every partial or symbolic representation, that reality is the reward of the seeker. The priority of reality to man's grasp is the foundation of Paul's dictum: Test everything; hold fast that which is good. Holding fast to that which is good is called faith or religion or commitment or heroism; testing every understanding of God, especially one's one, that understanding itself may be corrected and increased, is called skepticism.

The First Epistle of John clearly teaches the same double necessity: "Beloved, believe not every spirit, but try the spirits whether they are of God: because many false prophets are gone out into the world" (I John 4:1). God demands and rewards man's search. By every man's under-

standing of God he must, and does, live. He must therefore "try the spirits"—to distinguish truth from error, lest
error consume him and all men.

In the Sermon on the Mount, Jesus demanded that his
disciples distinguish the true prophet from the false:

> Beware of false prophets, which come to you in sheep's
> clothing, but inwardly they are ravening wolves.
> Ye shall know them by their fruits. Do men gather
> grapes of thorns, or figs of thistles?
> Even so every good tree bringeth forth good fruit; but
> a corrupt tree bringeth forth evil fruit.
> A good tree cannot bring forth evil fruit, neither can a
> corrupt tree bring forth good fruit.
> Every tree that bringeth not forth good fruit is hewn
> down, and cast into the fire.
> Wherefore by their fruits ye shall know them.
> Not everyone that saith unto me, Lord, Lord, shall en-
> ter the kingdom of heaven; but he that doeth the
> will of my Father which is in heaven.
>
> —Matthew 7:15–21

Jesus assumed the priority of reality to every man's understanding, including his own. "My Father is greater than
I," he said (John 14:28). "The Father that dwelleth in me,
he doeth the works" (John 14:10). Always he called attention to the fact that he had not sent the Father, but the
Father had sent him. "The servant is not greater than his
lord; neither he that is sent greater than he that sent him"
(John 13:16). Jesus assumed that God, who sustains and
necessitates man's search, participates to some degree in
every man's understanding. "He that hath seen me hath
seen the Father" (John 14:9). He understood his Father's
nature and demand as responsibility or love, for all men
in all lands and all ages; to all Christians, and to many
sincere fellow travelers, he remains the living incarnation,
in life and death, of the Father's character and will. God
is so important that he lends his importance to man's un-

derstanding; man must follow the idea of God he finds convincing. Christians are folk who find the nature and demand of the *macrocosm* in the *microcosm,* of the large in the small, of the One in the one; who see God in Christ, and take upon themselves his name and yoke, his call to responsible love—in every dimension of existence.

God Is Both a Skeptic and a Man of Faith

Skepticism and faith are required in man because they are the activities of God. Man must exercise himself to separate what is true from what is false, that he may live and grow, that he may worship God in truth as well as in spirit. Man must endlessly commit his strength to the good as he understands it, that he may not live and die in vain. God requires both testing and commitment, for he himself is everlastingly committed to human good and endlessly sifts all things. God is on the side of the real, the true, and the sane, and forever against the unreal, the untrue, and the insane. God condemns the false and confirms the true, and thus performs his creative task through, in spite of, and for human freedom, which is also his creation. God judges civilizations and souls at every moment, yet strengthens rather than cancels human freedom. Our freedom operates within a context of responsibility—not outside but inside unconditional divine sovereignty. God is great enough to sustain human freedom while correcting it, teaching it, leading it toward fulfillment, toward universal freedom and faithfulness in fellowship. In God's teaching process, which we call time and history, the unreal, the untrue, and the insane endlessly destroy themselves; there is no permanence in them. The world is a playground, but the playground is attached to a school; the school is a training center for athletes and the course is tough, for it is constructed to bring forth the best in every man for the sake of all men. Wartime training of U.S.

Marines had its moments of play, but the course was tough enough to make men curse, yet not as tough as the foe. God is totally committed to man, to man's growth toward the full stature of Christ in the soul, and the full fellowship of love in society. He is active to sustain the good of human freedom, even when that good is perverted and becomes the strength of evil. At the same time, God plays the role of the skeptic; he cuts away the crippling and uncreative so that freedom may breathe and learn. He is the enemy of every human claim of finality in structure and infallibility in truth—whether made by popes or dictators —for the claim destroys what it seeks to preserve. He is the foe of every human absolute, including the negative absolute of dogmatic irreligion.

The divine skeptic is the judge of men and nations, the analyst of the total content of time and history. The divine faithfulness, which sustains man in thought and life, is patient, but not too patient, with the human race, enrolled singly and altogether in the school of history; the divine faithfulness demands whole commitment to what man sees to be good, and whole criticism—in word and war —of what man sees to be evil. Divine skepticism is the Last Judgment at every moment in life and history, the final, inescapable, and supreme court from whose decisions there is no appeal. The divine faithfulness—in both commitment and criticism—is our salvation, the invasion of our clay with creating love. The divine skepticism and the divine commitment form one faithfulness, the nature and demand of God, the grace that is sufficient for man and the world, sufficient to bring freedom to historical fulfillment.

God, who is prior to our grasp, endlessly sustains our search, endlessly demands our finest commitment and our noblest criticism. God, who is unfailingly faithful, is our discipline and our delight, our judgment and our redemption.

We Do Not Possess God; He Possesses Us

God gives himself into our hands, sustains our use and abuse of his love, yet is never our possession. We can and do manipulate his world for our own ends: rich men grow richer; poor men grow angrier. Applied science manipulates energy in the service of material need. Prayer manipulates energy in the service of needs both material and spiritual; the highest form of prayer surrenders itself to be manipulated by all-powerful purpose. God possesses, sustains, and summons both science and prayer to the better and the more. Our governments manipulate God's world and often assume themselves its proprietors; yet our governments do not own the universe—they are owned, sustained, and judged by it. Our social classes and races manipulate reality and often assume private lordship over it; yet they are possessed, sustained, and summoned to creative fellowship by a greater Lord.

God both sustains and corrects us: sustained but not corrected, we could never find the way; corrected but not sustained, we would quickly perish.

Our manipulation *of* reality is the grace of freedom; our manipulation *by* reality is the fact of sovereignty. God possesses and in many ways coerces us—to seek bread for the body and wine for the soul, to seek neither unhappy holiness nor unholy happiness but holy happiness, the wholeness of universal brotherhood, the wholeness of usefulness and joy. Our freedom is predestined, sustained, corrected, and confirmed by reality. Our freedom exists within sovereignty, our free will within predestination. We are predestined to live, to be free, yet within the responsible call to fellowship; we are predestined to walk and work with God toward abundant life for all men, or to walk with unreality toward oblivion. God predestines through and for freedom the final fulfillment—one world of fellowship in faithfulness. As individuals we may refuse to be creative, refuse to work with God, refuse to contribute to whole-family fellowship, but our private refusal has no power to stop the steadfast movement toward fulfillment. If we insist, as individuals and nations, we may destroy ourselves, may excommunicate ourselves from God; we cannot destroy his forward movement through and for all men. God never excommunicates us; it is we who excommunicate ourselves. Death is neither more nor less than the fact of our finitude; we—individually—are not the whole of reality. The second death is the moral death we choose in life —our refusal of the great Invitation to faithful freedom. Our refusal illustrates the process; it can prevent neither its operation nor its achievement. As nations and civilizations we may refuse whole-family responsibility or love; our refusal only teaches later men the necessity of responsible love, the demand of creative faithfulness. Whole-family fellowship across this earth is on the agenda and cannot be prevented. God coerces the exercise of our freedom, our terrible choice of creativity or cowardice, the great Acceptance, which includes the acceptance of ourselves, or the great Refusal.

Our manipulation by reality toward whole-family fellowship is the creativity called righteousness; our manipulation of reality toward nationalism and egoism is the uncreativity called sin. Sin is not merely uncreative; it is positively destructive and its end is tragedy. God utilizes our good, sterilizes our evil; beyond the self-destruction of the false is the permanence of the true.

Energy is the body of God, purpose his spirit. The gift of energy makes our freedom real, our pilgrimage serious, our identity distinct. Fellowship is possible only among free and distinct persons who may use or abuse public institutions called bodies in a public place called the earth. The gift of energy provides our bodies and our earth—to make possible our fellowship as persons. Energy is the bearer and instrument of purpose; it exists within and for the will of God. Scientists have often denied that purpose exists within energy; they have never denied, as scientists, that energy exists within purpose. The gift of energy evolves the tools of fellowship; the gift of purpose creates the interplay of persons. Energy provides the means; purpose is, and creates, the end—the universal fellowship of persons across the earth and the ages. The means exist for and within the end.

We do not possess God; he possesses us both inwardly and outwardly. He possesses us inwardly because he sustains and necessitates the exercise of our freedom; he possesses us outwardly because he surrounds our freedom with a context of responsibility. He enters into direct fellowship with our freedom only with our consent. This creative fellowship (*koinonia*) Christians call "the baptism of the Holy Spirit." The Spirit is holy—for it is community-forming; it creates mutuality; it gathers all our human fragments into one whole-family fellowship; it quickens responsibility; it builds wholeness and usefulness and joy. *Agape* is God's love for man and the world; *eros* is man's love for the highest and best that he knows; where *agape* and *eros* meet, there is *koinonia*—creative fellowship.

God sustains and summons us, not to pride or lust or indifference, not to self-centered idolatry, not to self-righteousness, faithlessness, and cynicism, but to wholeness in our happiness and holiness in our goal, to the whole family of man in the fellowship of responsible love.

God is our security and our song. Our hope lies in the fact that God is prior to our search, greater than our grasp, the strength of our seeking and finding, the author and architect of the better that is on its way to us from the future. Our hope lies in the fact that God, who is both the push of life and the pull of love, is efficient in power and sufficient in purpose. Our whole-family pilgrimage will not end in failure. God is prior to our love, sustains, requires, and transcends our love, shines through and in

spite of our self-love, is the critic of our lovelessness. The
God who possesses us is Love.

Think We Must

Well-meaning people have at times felt that human reason, an untrustworthy tool, leads inevitably to atheism.
They have believed that man's reason is man's enemy, and
therefore the enemy of God. They have sought to evade
the rational nature and demand of God by an ascent to
mysticism or a descent to romanticism.

Mysticism is both a power and a problem: when it
seeks the face of God and listens intently to his word and
will, it releases the power of God unto salvation; when it
seeks escape from reason's strenuous responsibility, it is
a problem to faith and to life. Prayer—one form of mysticism—is inevitable in human experience: all men pray, in
some degree, at every crisis in their lives, because man is
not God; at the end of every experiment in self-sufficiency
is self-despair. Prayer at its best is the full commitment of
human reason to learn, and of human strength to do, the
will of God. Prayer, however, like every other gift, can be
misused. It is rightly used when it opens human life to the
invasion of healing and creating grace; it is thus the self-
transcendence of reason. It is wrongly used when it seeks
escape from reason itself, when it attempts to bypass man's
necessary struggle to see. As an avenue of escape, mysticism
is hypocrisy; it asserts in practice what it denies in theory.
It pretends to discount human reason in its search for revelation; yet, in fact, it is itself an exercise of human reason;
the mystic inevitably carries with him into prayer the
conception of God reason has given him. The true mystic
perceives that God is more than the picture presented by
reason; he presses on into the fellowship of prayer that he
may know God, the Other and the Near, for himself, with
less and less distortion. As long as he remains a true mystic,
he will not deceive himself—will not deny the participa-

tion of his own mind and heart in prayer. Not in escape from reason but through and beyond its conclusions, true mysticism seeks the face of God. False mysticism seeks God through escape from reason, not through reason but around it, and thus ignores the speech of God to and in reason.

The exercise of human reason is a form of work; it is painful and responsible, and the possibility of error is legion. Man's finest wisdom must allow a margin of uncertainty. False mysticism—the attempt to avoid the hard work of reason—is inertia, sluggishness of mind, and hence a form of disobedience. Every disobedience produces strange distortions. The false mystic may develop an ecstatic feeling that he is no longer man but God; he may forget his creaturely status as a man in the hand of God; he may succumb to spiritual pride, to the fiction that he alone possesses God. Mary Baker Eddy has convinced thousands that man's enemy is the false belief that his mind is mortal. Paul urged man to put off the carnal mind, to put on the spiritual mind; he urged men not to forget but to remember that their minds were mortal, less than the mind of God. Mrs. Eddy confused the mortal mind with the carnal mind. Indeed, the two are often confused in all personal experience. Yet the two are not identical. One is not sinful because his mind is the mind of a man, a mortal mind; sin begins when he forgets that he is a creature of God, that his mind is mortal. The carnal mind is sinful because it dedicates good energy to evil purpose, perverts legitimate desire into illegitimate lust. The mortal mind as such is not sinful; it is man himself, thinking and acting as man. The mortal mind cannot fully comprehend the mind of God, but without the full exercise of mortal mind, man can comprehend nothing.

The ascent to mysticism sometimes becomes, in the event, a descent below reason. Man starts with the firm conviction that he is rising above his fellow men, but finds to his dismay, when he returns to sanity, that he has fallen below them. He looks down with contempt upon those who struggle with the slow processes of reason, yet at the last he must offer grateful thanks to those who have struggled—and paid the price of common gain. Pacifism can be a firm work of reason, for most of our wars are shining examples of social insanity. Some pacifists, however, have been known to look down from their lofty height upon the struggle of free men against tyranny; the same men, at a later date, have offered humble thanks that tyranny was overthrown.

More common than mysticism is the descent from reason called romanticism. Romanticism and mysticism are distinct, yet very much alike, and often in practice indistinguishable. Romanticism considers reason quaint and sterile, and it succumbs with wild abandon to the thrust of emotion. The gospel of romanticism is this: do not criticize your impulses; obey them. Romanticism, of course, adds to as well as subtracts from the common good. When reason declares that our natural desires are sinful, it is too unreasonable to be helpful. Men who have sought to exclude emotion from reason have found themselves, and their conclusions, sterile. When reason denies that reality includes emotion, it offers man an arid desert. A man may build a philosophy through the exercise of reason, but find at the last no place in the system for life, even his own. The man of reason may know that logic is a straight line but forget that life is a curve, and in his haste to draw a straight line he eliminates the curve altogether. When this occurs, a new outburst of romanticism is inevitable. Every John Knox is followed by a Bobby Burns. God is in our bodies as well as our minds. The call of hunger, for food or sex or play, is not a perversion; it is not immoral; it is the thrust of energy, seeking with purpose for fulfillment. Drive without direction is anarchy and tragedy; it makes fulfillment impossible: this is the weakness of romanticism.

It surrenders to the thrust of emotion but cannot steer a course between anarchy and tyranny; it has rejected at the start the critical or steering faculty of the mind; having rejected reason, it cannot, without acknowledging error, call upon it in the hour of need. The romanticist becomes, at best, a man of quiet self-indulgence, or, at worst, an enthusiast for Hitler or his kind—a noisy supporter of any leader who surrenders principle to passion. This misuse of passion is always the perversion of principle, for passion without principle is blind.

It is inevitable, at times, that men will seek escape from reason through the ascent of mysticism or the descent of romanticism, yet the very desire to escape is a testimony to reason's strong demand. God has so constructed man that he must strive to separate the adequate from the inadequate, and the present conclusions of reason, including one's own, often demonstrate their inadequacy in public. The priority of God thrusts upon man the necessary search for the adequate; and this is only another way of saying that God, who is prior to man, is rational.

Try as we will to escape the exercise of human reason, we only illustrate its necessity by the sorrow of our departure. The very speed of our search for escape bears witness to our dissatisfaction with every substitution of a lie for the truth. We are in flight from ourselves, from our own demand for rational integrity, when we pursue either false mysticism or false romanticism. True mysticism is the realization that God is more than our understanding; true romanticism is the realization that God is more than our emotion. Think we must, whether our thoughts participate in whole or in part, or not at all, in reality. We are what we think; for what we think, we do, and what we think, we love.

Every man is the walking image of his thought. If our thought is white superiority, we are Nazis. If our thought is the right of the worker to rule everybody for his own good, we are Communists. If our thought is the right of isolation from the world into the private nightmare of American self-interest, we are stateside hysterical nationalists. To think like a Christian is to believe that universal brotherhood is required in man because responsible love is the nature of God.

There is, then, no final distinction between thought and faith. What we think is what we believe; what we believe is what we think—in science, in political economy, in ethics, in class and race relations, and therefore in religion, which embraces them all. No gain is made by any attempt to escape human reason. We can live only by what we think is true, whether we are wits or half-wits, whether our thought is sense or nonsense.

Human reason can never exhaust the truth of God; there is, however, a self-correcting activity within human reason—the activity called skepticism. Pride of intellect has risen only when human reason has failed to perceive the priority of God to its conclusions. Our trouble is not that we have thought too much but that we have thought too little, and have failed to see that God, who is stronger than we are, will never let us rest, never leave us content, with any prematurity.

The Pathetic Fallacy—Dogmatism

There are two basic miscarriages of human reason: the first is the assumption of infallibility, what Toynbee calls the "pathetic" fallacy; the second is the assumption that no relation exists between reason and reality, what Toynbee calls the "apathetic" fallacy. Where the assumption of finality begins, growth stops, and with it creativity. In religious terms, the assumption of finality in any human thought is idolatry, even when, or especially when, human thought is religious. Nothing precedes God, though many things make the attempt. "Thou shalt have no other gods before me"—not even a human representation of God. Our conception of reality is always less than reality. Revelation is the speech of reality to man, but what reality speaks and what man hears are not identical. In the act of hearing what God declares, what we bring with us to the audience conditions, distorts, and relativizes every word that we hear—whether we listen as atheists or fundamentalists. Whatever we think, there is a slight gap between our truth and the truth. Not to see or not to acknowledge the existence of this gap is the cause and curse of dogmatism—whether in science, philosophy, or religion.

The Apathetic Fallacy—Relativism

If one deadly enemy of growth is dogmatism—the denial that God is more than our thought—the other deadly enemy is relativism—the denial that reality is rational or coherent. If dogmatism makes growth impossible, relativism makes growth meaningless. Absolute relativism is a contradiction in terms; the word "absolute" can hardly be used by men committed to relativity. Many an excited relativist has declared: "There are no absolutes." The statement is its own denial; one absolute is asserted. It is one thing to maintain that truth is more than our grasp of it; it is quite another to take seriously the view that there is nothing to take seriously, that no distinction is valid between sense and nonsense. A farmer said to William James: "There isn't much difference between men, but what difference there is is very important." The difference between creative and uncreative ideas is not less so.

In all probability there are no simon-pure relativists; the so-called relativist must live and work—like the rest of us; he must earn a salary and support his family; he must pay alimony to one or more ex-wives if he has been "relatively" faithful to one. The actual working relativist, whether simon-pure or simon-simple, is common enough in our generation: he is strongly committed to one absolute, his own immediate self-interest; to him all other values are relative—that is, less than A-1 priorities. If the working relativist were to become an absolute relativist, he would surrender the last absolute, his own self-interest, the last link with reality.

Dogmatism, like skepticism, considers truth important, worth fighting and dying, even living, for. But dogmatism confuses, equates, and identifies its understanding of truth with the whole of truth; it can thus never progress toward a clearer comprehension of truth. The so-called absolute relativist is, in fact, an absolute dogmatist; he too refuses the summons to growth. Partial relativism rightly recognizes the fallibility in every man's grasp of truth; it is therefore tolerant of a wide variety of opinion; it is not afraid of difference of opinion. But partial relativism tends to consider truth itself an illusion; if truth is not more than a mirage, man's ascent from darkness is ended. The so-called ascent from darkness is neither more nor less than a man walking in circles in the desert at midnight.

Somewhere between dogmatism and relativism is the life and growth of reason. For this reason, "faith at war with skepticism" is not good enough for man. Because dogmatism assumes finality in present thought, it frustrates growth. Because relativism assumes that no human thought participates in reality, it paralyzes the nerve of growth; *arthritis* becomes complete. To think at all is to believe that one's thought, however limited, actually participates in the real, the true, and the sane. Acceptance of the summons to growth makes a man an ex-dogmatist and an ex-relativist at the same instant; he realizes, with new humility, that clearer thought will increase his degree of participation.

Dogmatism and relativism are liabilities in the world of ethics. The moral law is the demand of God upon us all. The moral code is our understanding of the moral law; it is always less than the law it interprets. Ethical dogmatism requires universal obedience to a moral code rather than to the moral law. Ethical relativism announces, as an infallible faith, that moral codes never correspond to reality, that no moral law shines above and through the moral code, that the moral code is not an imperfect representation of reality but the perfect representation of unreality, the face not of fact but of fiction.

Relativism in the pursuit of truth declares: "There is no truth to pursue." Relativism in ethics asserts: "There is no moral law." The moral code of the relativist is "Anything goes." The moral law for the relativist is his own survival, and this, even to him, becomes less and less important. Expediency may be either moral or immoral. When a man attempts to apply the moral law, as he understands it, to immediate situations, to concrete daily behavior, he is forced to practice moral expediency; when he recognizes no moral law, he can practice only immoral expediency, the service of immediate self-interest. When a man has constructed a moral code to his present satisfaction and fully grasps the fact that the moral law transcends it, he must still decide how to apply the code to the present problem. He must fall back on some "rule of thumb"; he must use the principle of expediency, the effort to apply broad principles to narrow situations. If he is committed to the moral law, he will apply his moral code with some margin for error, that is, with some tolerance of diverse opinions, some respect for differing moral codes. He will know, when he has acted as ethically as possible, that his action has participated in the good, but not fully. He may have accepted the call of *inviolate truth* but rejected the call of *complete concern*.

Immoral expediency is the practice of the man who believes himself confronted with no ethical demand—no summons to inviolate truth, no subpoena to complete concern. Immoral expediency is another term for ethical paralysis. Men often fail to be moral even when they are trying to be. When a man concludes that no moral law commands his responsible behavior, he stops trying—except as a habit inherited from childhood. Heroism is the attempt to be moral in the immediate; immoral expediency is full surrender to the push and pull of desire, the end of heroism, the end of man, the beginning of madness.

Responsible marriage, to cite but one example, has suffered in our time from ethical dogmatism, but even more from ethical relativism. Faithfulness is required in marriage, as in a business partnership, in a parent-child relation, or in the pursuit of whole-family fellowship throughout the earth. Both the height of humor and depth of tragedy are reached when an ethical dogmatist marries an ethical relativist. To say the least, the two find themselves out of step. The ethical absolutist, for example, may conclude prematurely that faithfulness, the moral law, is not more than the law against adultery. He may be faithless to his wife in other ways with good conscience; he may be critical, suspicious, penurious. The ethical relativist, by definition, concludes that there is no moral law, no demand for faithfulness in the nature of reality; as long as self-interest, whether financial or sexual, is served, she will remain faithful—but no longer. The ethical absolutist avoids adultery as he avoids the plague. The ethical relativist, in time of stress and strain, accepts adultery as she accepts food and drink from other tables than her own.

Shall the adultery of the ethical relativist bring the marriage to an end? If the moral law of faithfulness is not more than the single commandment against adultery, the marriage is ended. These personalities, united by mutual interest, were never a community of whole responsibility to begin with; this marriage, if made in heaven, is consummated in hell. However, if the moral law of faithfulness includes the commandment against adultery, but includes also the commandment of forgiveness and new venture, the husband who so perceives it will seek his wife's conversion, and his own, to creative faithfulness. Hosea sought the conversion of Gomer, his adulterous wife; he described God as one who remains faithful to man—through and beyond man's faithlessness.

You have three things to consider: the moral law, faithfulness, the nature and demand of God; the specific moral code which excludes adultery; and a specific act of adultery on the part of a woman who believes that the demand for faithfulness has no root in reality. The commandment against adultery participates in but does not exhaust the law of faithfulness; the seventh commandment is one of ten. If the reader believes that the commandment against adultery is the whole of the moral law, he will vote for immediate divorce in the case described above. If the reader believes that there is no moral law, that the commandment against adultery is an illusion, has he accepted his own marriage vows with sincerity?

Here, whether or not hereafter, the alternative to hell is not heaven but purgatory. The faithless wife is still a subject of redemption; she may yet learn that God places the demand of faithfulness upon her. For the present she is something other than an inspiration to her husband. No permanence in marriage can be built upon her. The only promise of permanence in this marriage is the husband's faithfulness, itself much less than whole. Only around faithfulness, the moral law, can adultery be overcome and a broken marriage be rebuilt—enriched by creative fellowship.

Ethical dogmatism makes marriage difficult; ethical relativism makes marriage impossible. Beyond both is faithfulness, the nature and demand of God, the only hope for the relativist in this world and the one light which is greater than dogmatism. God, who lays upon man the demand of responsibility, the demand of faithfulness, is expedient without expediency, and prudent without prudery.

Ethics involves the final achievement of freedom and faithfulness in fellowship across all mankind; it is therefore universal as well as personal. Often enough, men think of ethics only in personal terms. The command of faithfulness is the basis of personal sanity, but also the basis of world community—the only possible foundation of a permanent fellowship of nations.

To see clearly and to act responsibly are our impossible possibilities—our impossible but imperative commands. Our seeing and acting are never adequate, yet they are always our opportunities for increased participation in reality—for increased fellowship with God and man. It all adds up to one conclusion: adequate religion, the insistent call of God, cannot appear when faith is at war with skepticism, at war with its own demand.

Skepticism: The Ally of Faith

IN THEOLOGY and religion, as in international relations, most of our noisier wars have been unnecessary. They have occurred only because the deeper basis of reconciliation was not perceived, or, if perceived, was rejected. When once it is grasped that one God confronts man in revelation and in reason, the long war between orthodoxy and rationalism will be seen to be obsolete.

Suffering is often the price of insight. Through much struggle I came to pre-skeptical religion. Through more struggle I came to pre-skeptical irreligion. Through ten years of atheism, and the struggle of graduate study, I came to post-skeptical faith—regarded, prematurely, as the quiet harbor of life, the end of the search.

Mature Faith and Skepticism

A new step in understanding has likewise come through struggle, as a college professor attempting to interpret constructive religion to American youth, but even more as a student of contemporary theology. My two-volume study of living American theologians (*Major Voices in American Theology*, 1953; and *Men Who Shape Belief*, 1955. Philadelphia: Westminster Press) was to me a glorious adventure. The second volume advanced with greater clarity an insight presented in the first: the realization that time and history are inside, not outside, the purpose and power of God. In preparing these volumes I read with care and love everything in print by twenty contemporary interpreters of religion. This struggle with diverse systems of belief opened a new dimension in skepticism and a new dimension in faith. Slowly enough the realization has grown, and is still growing, that in the service of God and fully within his will for us, skepticism is always faith's necessary ally.

The careful reader will ask at this point: "Is your present position final?" No human thinking is final; man's mind never fully grasps the mind of God. God's will is always better than and greater than our understanding. God presents every man, every age, and every stage in thought with the insistent demand of growth, with the joyful invitation to fuller fellowship.

The struggle with the ideas of twenty living theologians has produced, as you would expect, a measure of growth, a rethinking of settled convictions. In two pivotal areas, above others, change has occurred: in the "how" (epistemology) and the "what" (ontology) of all human knowledge —when skepticism and faith are taken seriously, with neither watered down, when skepticism is understood not as faith's enemy but as faith's ally and friend. Skepticism cannot operate until, pending better sight, faith commits itself to what it perceives to be true. Faith is not credulity, but commitment to the highest and best that are presently perceived. Faith is practical, not absolute, certainty—pending further investigation. Skepticism is man's perpetually necessary endeavor to distinguish the real from the unreal. Paul, as we have seen, understood that we must "test all things, and hold fast to that which is good." Skepticism and faith, laboring thus together, form the actual content of the scientific method, and at the same time the actual content of the religious method. What is false must be distinguished and destroyed; what is true must be discerned and upheld. Skepticism and faith, criticism and commitment, are perpetual necessities—to ordinary men and women as well as scientists, philosophers, and saints. No man can really afford to abandon either activity. When men cast away faith—whole commitment to what they regard as real—skepticism is finished; commitment to what is seen to be true is the strength of all criticism of what is seen to be false. When men cast away skepticism, faith atrophies and becomes blind commitment to unexamined principles, blind obedience to pope or tyrant, hysterical conformity to nationalism, to religious or irreligious dogmatism. Put differently, faith without skepticism is idolatry; it claims infallibility in its grasp of truth, an infallibility not in its possession. No one can search for truth when convinced that no truth awaits discovery. Unless man acts upon truth as he sees it, till better truth appears, the good cannot be tested, the better cannot appear. Skepticism without faith is a false absolute; absolute skepticism is not skepticism but a new infallibility—an absolute commitment exempt from searching scrutiny. If no truth exists, whether in or beyond man's grasp, the search, without reason for existence, must wither and die. Skepticism purges faith and must do so forever; faith sustains and necessitates skepticism while it builds the better and the more in the world and in the soul. An Oxford University scientist put it this way: "Faith is more important than skepticism—at least in the short run; in my laboratory I get nowhere with a project unless I believe it to be terribly important. Later, skeptical scrutiny may alter my belief, but without the starting and sustaining impulse of faith, skepticism would have nothing to work on."

No truth that man discovers is equal to the truth that sustains and requires the discovery. Truth is prior to man's search for it. From the truth that God is and requires has come man's ability to distinguish, if only in part, the real from the unreal as the basis of action—politically, socially, economically, religiously, ethically, and personally. In Christian terms, God is both the energy of the world and the Lord of the world's energy; God thus conceived is prior to the search which discovers him; his speech to man is prior to man's understanding or misunderstanding of the speech. Revelation is prior to the activity of human reason, yet not at war with it. Revelation, the communication of reality to man, sustains man's skepticism and man's faith, and summons both to a better walk with God, a firmer commitment to his work in and for the world.

Growth is clear in my understanding of the "how" of knowledge, but what of my understanding of the "what" —the structure of reality, the nature of God? Theologians are increasingly aware that two halves of one blunder are evident—alike in secular and religious thought. On the one hand are the otherworldly, preoccupied with the eternal above and beyond time and history; on the other are the this-worldly, concerned with time and history but emptying them of eternal meaning and demand. Half the world thinks of eternity and relegates time to meaninglessness; the other half thinks of time and relegates its eternal meaning and summons to the status of an illusion. Increasingly the realization grows that energy and purpose are the structure of God, the content of reality, and therefore the strength and goal of all time and all history—that the world as we know it exists to become the full incarnation of the divine purpose. From birth to death, and whether we are atheists or saints, we live and learn *within* the energy and purpose of God; we exist, as civilizations and as individual men, to be transfigured, transformed, completed in faithful fellowship. The purpose of all life and all history is fulfillment.

Purpose has created energy to bear the human pilgrimage toward fulfillment. Purpose does not inhabit an isolated world disjoined from energy; energy and purpose are joined together in God; what God hath joined together let no man put asunder. Energy and purpose are not at war—else God is a split personality. From first to last, energy exists within purpose; in H. Richard Niebuhr's expression: "The world of culture, man's achievement, exists within the world of Grace, God's Kingdom" (*Christ and Culture.* New York: Scribner's, 1951, p. 256). The present exists within and for the future; this world moves within and for the world that is to come—in time and history. All that is, in our troubled and confused pilgrimage, is on its inevitable way *forward,* in the care and control of all-powerful Love, to one world of freedom and faithfulness in fellowship.

To me, therefore, Christianity is true; it is a divine call, not a human achievement; its true content is its call to faithful freedom. It is always a gift, though sometimes slowly received. Its structure of belief is clear: all life is the presence of energy and purpose, the presence of God; responsibility or love is his nature and demand, the character and gift of the Holy Spirit, the summons to growth made flesh in the Church's understanding of Jesus as the Christ; in him responsibility or love, "to all men, for all men, and for everything," remained true to itself—before the Cross, on the Cross, and from the Cross forward forever. To this responsibility all men and all human institutions are called. Our churches do not possess love; love possesses and judges our churches, and sometimes shatters our self-love. Love sustains not the church only, but the total life of the world—all classes and conditions of men. God is our school and our teacher, and we learn as nations and religions and men—but slowly, as befits our status as creatures and scholars. God is stronger than our man-made gods and will not be denied. Every man is called to be a son of God; the whole family of man is called to be the image of God. God coerces our experiment with life, our matriculation in the school of the present; he invites and constrains us to learn our lessons, to unite honest skepticism with honest faith—to test all things, to hold fast that which is good: in politics, in religion, in ethics, in economics, and in social practice. God participates in, yet transcends, all our seeking and finding. The pilgrimage is not folly, but growing fulfillment—in the world and in the soul—not without tragedy, for judgment is God's skepticism of our proud inadequacies, but through and beyond tragedy. Faith is heroism; skepticism, which separates heroic truth from heroic error, is hard work; but now as always faith without works is dead.

The Psychological Priority of Our Attempt to See

Too long we of the orthodox trinitarian tradition have labeled "unitarian" every attempt of human reason to understand the speech of reality to man. Hard-thinking rationalists have suspected that we are afraid of the white light of reason, that perhaps we have something to hide. If in any degree we have been fearful, we need be so no longer. Not two Gods, but one God confronts us in revelation and in reason. God is not afraid of human thought; he fears, for our sake, only the absence of it; he endlessly invites every man to begin where he is.

"Just as I am, without one plea"—runs a line from an old hymn. Embedded in the words is an obvious fact: every man must wrestle with God where and as he meets him. No man can start where he is not. An American citizen meant to be helpful but was not overly relevant in his advice to a tourist: "If I were you, I wouldn't start from here." Sweet idealists are always telling us the same thing.

It is also true that every man must start. Live we must; our lives are the motion pictures of our principles. Our central assignment, no matter where we begin, is to see life steadily and see it whole, to serve God to the best of our ability, and to enjoy him forever.

Much preaching, however well-intended, evades the central issue. The pulpit command "Repent, and believe" is sound enough, but meaningless until the hearer perceives that he has fallen below the demand of God—the practice of responsibility or love. Until a man sees for himself the demand of God, he cannot perceive that he has fallen below it; the command "Repent, and believe the gospel" is the sound of a hammer on cold iron. The iron must be heated to be malleable. To hammer on cold metal is to create nothing but noise. The artist, hammering on white-hot metal, may bend it to his will. Much preaching hammers noisily on cold metal because it evades the question: "What must I do to be saved?" Ancient texts sometimes reveal, sometimes obscure, the faithful freedom which is God's nature, demand, and gift. It was said in the time of Samuel that until he came, there was no frequent vision; Samuel's time and ours have much in common. Men go to church to hear the voice of God, but sometimes hear only the echo of their own voices. When the voice of God does speak in our churches, the self-conscious intellectual is not there to listen. Only the humble hear and are glad. Preaching is an indispensable power when it enables the hearer to see God for himself, and thus to see wherein he has fallen below the faithfulness which God is, requires, and gives to all who will receive.

It is customary in this century to dismiss Descartes with scorn, yet his emphasis upon individual integrity of thought is the need of our collectivist century. To be sure, life does not begin with my thought about it; life is prior to my thought. Insofar as Descartes left the impression that nothing exists except the thinking ego, he has proven more harmful than helpful. Yet his insistence that a man must begin where he is, must think what he cannot help but think, is simple honesty.

God was here before I was born, before I began to think for myself. Yet the priority of God to my thought in no way exempts me from the painful or joyful necessity of thinking. God makes my thought possible; he has pro-

duced the world as it is, and me as I am; he requires and
sustains my effort, yet I must begin where I am with such
knowledge as is available to me, well-mixed, as always,
with ignorance.

Psychologically, therefore, the attempt to see is primary.
This is the reason a twenty-year-old often regards all he
learned at sixteen as beneath his dignity. As well as his
parents could, they taught him all they knew; it was little
enough, and not all of it was true. His parents taught him
what they knew at forty; the son learned it when he was
less than sixteen. At twenty, he feels himself beyond it; he
considers what he learned earlier in life, everything his
parents hold dear, as pre-literate. The twenty-year-old
often looks down on his parents. This does not mean that
parents know less than their sons. It may mean only that
sons never understand what their parents try to teach
them. It means in any case that every man's attempt to see,
to know, to understand, is not of secondary importance.
Wise men always listen with respect to young ideas, however immature.

In point of fact, the son may be centuries behind his
parents. As Mark Twain put it: "When I was fourteen, I
considered my father very ignorant. But at twenty-one I
was amazed to see how much the old man had learned in
seven years." Life and truth are gifts of one God, yet we
often meet them separately. Psychologically speaking,
truth is one thing, life another. At twenty, a youth cannot
accept what he learned at ten, no matter how weighty the
cited authorities. At thirty he may discover that his own
growing understanding bears a striking likeness to what
his parents taught him—if for no other reason than that
his parents, and himself, are wrestling with the same world.
At twenty he is, and must be, on his own. God requires
that every youth come to terms with truth and sanity for
himself. God draws every youth into close-range wrestling.
Parents can, and must, teach their children as much as

their children will learn. Parents must also learn to stand aside, with silent prayer or hand wringing, when God draws their child toward individual encounter. God is a better teacher than any parent—when youth asserts independence. God can be trusted. He will sustain the youth's first halting efforts to use his own mind; he will not frown upon a youth's ecstatic belief that he has discovered truths never seen before. God will inflate a youth's pride, then deflate it, without destroying his freedom, that he may grow in wisdom and stature, content with no human finality. God, in time, will teach a youth self-sufficiency, self-determination, and self-direction in thought and life; he will then teach him self-despair at the end of self-sufficiency, and beyond despair, creative fellowship with and for all men. Parents must not become idolaters, road blocks between God and their child. God will move parents aside, whether they are proud or humble, that their child may see the sun. Parents can then rejoice with their child in his growing sight, or disown him because he prefers God to their god. God teaches parents as well as children—not to be idolaters, not to identify their understanding of God with God, but to live with confidence that God is fully adequate—for parents and children alike.

The Objective Priority of What Is to Be Seen

We must begin where we are, yet the God we seek to comprehend was here before we were born; he will be here after we die; he gives us life, drives us to the venture of skepticism and faith, and, if we are willing, to the greater venture of creative action with and for our fellow men.

Two thinkers in our time have occupied opposite horns of the same dilemma; they have emphasized two halves of one truth. Henry Nelson Wieman in all his books has asserted the psychological priority of our attempt to see. Karl Barth in all his books has asserted the objective priority of what is to be seen. The two systems of thought are not enemies but friends. Wieman perceives that we must wrestle with God on our own account—must seek his nature and demand. Barth perceives that God is greater than any human grasp. Both perceptions are essential. God is to be seen; he is there; yet our seeing is our necessity, for we live by what we see. We therefore pray for clearer sight as we live by the sight thus far given. God creates diverse witnesses and fills all the space between their ideas.

God Is Before, In, With, and Beyond Our Reason

Revelation is the speech of reality to man; man's reason is his comprehension of the speech. God who speaks *to* human reason existed before human reason, for the universe is older than man. God who speaks *in* human reason necessitates man's endless effort to separate sense from nonsense. God who speaks *in* human reason speaks both *to* and *with* man. "Come now, and let us reason together, saith the Lord" (Isaiah 1:18). Revelation, the conversation of God with man, is a dialogue, yet also a monologue. It is a monologue because God is prior to and greater than our comprehension; it is a dialogue because God demands our participation in the conversation, our attempt to see for ourselves. God sustains us while we learn, and in spite of our failure to learn aright. He is not always patient; rather he is coercive, and he can be nothing else. If we leap over a precipice, we crush our bodies on the rocks below. God is sovereign: he coerces the exercise of our freedom within a context of responsibility.

God, who is before us, who speaks in us, to us, and with us, is also beyond us. Our hope is better comprehension. History is the story of slow but increasing understanding. We no longer throw babies in the river; we no longer approve, in principle, of human slavery. We learn slowly, but we learn. The thing that makes our learning possible is the nature and demand of God—always beyond us, always greater than and better than our present comprehension. Our asset is greater than our liabilities. Our asset is God. Our liabilities are the gods we have made in our own image.

God is our asset in science; he sustains the scientist in his work, surrenders to his probing analysis, yields to his control, yet always breaks through in new dimensions beyond his grasp and thus keeps him at work. God is our asset in philosophy; he summons the philosopher to discover the relations between facts, which are fully as important as the facts themselves; he surrenders to the philosopher's understanding, and leaps forward beyond his conclusions. God is our asset in political life; he necessitates our constant pursuit of adequate government; he sustains our perpetual effort to reduce overgrown government to useful proportions; he makes us the critics of our government and our government our critic. God sustains our governments, surrenders to political manipulation, yet endlessly transcends our imperialism, our isolationism, our national egoism. God is our asset in economics; he sustains the farm, the factory, and the store; he lends his energy to management and labor alike, to the half-truth of unmitigated individualism in the West and the half-truth of unmitigated socialism in the East; transcending all economic classes and creeds, he summons all to one world. God is our asset in religion, in ethics, in education, and in social change; he demands our attention, sustains our half-finished enterprise, lends himself to our partialities, our racial divisions, our class discriminations, yet transcends our conflicts, our cleavages, our fragments, with the call to whole-family fellowship.

God was *before* the world in creation; God is the energy in the world, in the growing physical universe, in the whole evolutionary process, and in the total movement of human life out of the past, through the present, into the future; God is *with* the world in providence, in the vision of the saints of all religions, supremely in Jesus Christ, the incarnate speech of reality. The instrument of the speech was crucified; the speech remains. God is *with* the world in the Spirit and the Church, and in all un-Christian or non-Christian society which is the latent church, the church in preparation; and God is *beyond* the world, transcending our despair with hope.

God Is Always Creative—in Rejection or Acceptance

The enterprise of God is always creative, yet he rejects what is false—that the true may prevail. He encloses both life and truth in one enterprise; to him, a man is more important than his present unreality; a man is more important than his sin. A man needs time and space for his wrestle with reality; God guarantees his opportunity in the midst of failure and success. God is coercive, yet frustrates every human effort to place life in a strait jacket. He sets the conditions of life, which are truth and sanity; freedom operates with and within the conditions. God sustains man's freedom, even man's freedom to refuse—that freedom may learn to refuse the evil and choose the good. Not forever, but for long, God sustains unjust governments and unjust men—that governments and men may learn justice. History is strewn with the wreckage of proud nations that fell and of proud men that preferred private gain to public good. Not forever does God reason with individual man, but long enough to establish what freedom has chosen. God does not reason forever with civilizations, nations, and persons, but long enough to learn what is in them, long enough for them to learn what is in themselves, long enough to learn the good that is worth preserving. God does not reason forever with individual persons, civilizations, and nations; nonetheless, he has thus far reasoned, and will reason "forever," with the human race as a whole; the total enterprise cannot end in failure. At no time does God release his grasp of mankind. Failure in individual civilizations and souls has no power to stop the process, the wrestle of reality with man. Beyond the failure of individual civilizations and souls is the quickening of the learning process in the human race as a whole. Life moves on, though individuals perish. Our seventy-year conversation with God is one form of our participation in immortality. Our thousand-year existence as a civilization is our thousand-year wrestle with immortality. Life moves through freedom's rough detours and long delays—inevitably forward. The learning process is slow, yet freedom learns; only freedom can learn; God shepherds freedom toward responsible love.

Unreality has no permanence; the winds of God destroy the house on sand, ventilate the house on rock. Broad is the road of confusion and capitulation; narrow is the road of responsible freedom. The road to life is broad *quantitatively:* it sustains all manner of men and all men of manner, an indeterminate variety of languages, customs, religions, and institutions; for life is the gift of God which makes learning possible. The road to life is narrow *qualitatively,* for the real is not the unreal. As Goethe put it: "The fashion of this world passeth away, and I would fain occupy myself only with the abiding."

God matriculates man in the university and multiversity of life; with man's help, and against man's hindrance, he slowly but surely creates our world in his image. God accepts man as a candidate for creative maturity. For man's sake, God rejects man's untruth; he destroys, but not for the love of destruction. Every destructive act of God is creative: what is half-finished must be completed; what hinders completion must be cast away.

God Is on All Sides of Us

When skepticism is fully faithful, it becomes increasingly aware that the false has been sustained only by its mixture with the true, that man's clearer grasp of the true is the invitation and reward of God. Slowly perhaps but surely, the skeptic's wonder increases—not merely at the truth he sees, but even more at the truth beyond his sight. The skeptic comes slowly but surely to the realization that he has not sought the truth half as wholeheartedly as the truth has sought him—his mind, his heart, his enriched fellowship with the human race, his creative commitment to the future. The skeptic comes slowly to the view that all that seems purposeless in his own life and in the life of the world has been enclosed within purpose from the beginning, that purpose is not less than all that seems purposeless but more. What seems purposeless—the endless play of natural change—provides human freedom with a variety of choices, and thus makes freedom real; in no other way is learning possible.

The endeavor, however difficult, to separate the real from the unreal awakens the conviction that the real has driven the faithful skeptic to his task, that the nature and demand of God is truth and sanity, responsibility or love, across the earth and the ages. If the world is a tale told by an idiot, full of sound and fury, signifying nothing, there has been no point in the effort to find the sense in the sound, the fact in the fury.

If the skeptic concludes that purpose is an illusion, he is no longer a skeptic; he has experienced the driving purpose of skeptical action—to separate the real from the unreal—and must now deny it or consider it a form of intellectual play—the meaningless self-entertainment of a strangely sensitive clod in a vacuum. If this is the skeptic's infallible dogma—that reality is purposeless, that human choice is an event in Nowhere—reality will not let him rest with his conclusion. It will drive him on, as it has thus far driven him, till he discovers that he is more than a cipher in the sea.

The stars in their courses, the earth in its orbit, the rise and fall of empires and men, the long learning process of evolution, the short learning process of history—all that seems purposeless bears within it, and not without order, a driving and restless energy. To be a man is to be a free, purposing, and responsible being. Conscious purpose moves not only in man but also, in some degree, in animal; unconscious purpose moves in the interplay of chemical forces, the wedding and argument of proton and neutron in the atom. Man's life as an individual may or may not be filled with purpose, with master motive; it is always filled with purposes, the pursuit of values or possessions. When man stops purposing, he stops being a man. Purpose is the presence of God in man. To conclude that reality is purposeless is to deny what man has learned from nature, history, and his own life. If a man concludes that reality is purposeless, he will nevertheless go right on purposing; God, greater than his conception, will thrust him onward toward clearer understanding and nobler living.

One thing only keeps the skeptic at work: the realization that reality demands in him responsibility or love. It demands heroic effort to make the true prevail; it demands the conviction that reality is worth preserving, that in his effort to separate the untrue from the true he is working *with* reality, that reality is working *with* him, and *in* him, that he is not alone, that what is purposeless functions within the creative purpose of the Omnipotent Pedagogue. Skepticism can operate only as long as a man is convinced that the truth is more than his thought—that God is on all sides of him at every second and in every situation.

Purpose Is Prior to Process

The final measure of a thing is not its beginning but its end. The true estimate of a life is not its childhood but its maturity. One discovers the truth or untruth of a civilization not in its roots but its fruits. England, it is said, loses all the battles but the last. The skeptic, who believes so strongly in reality that he casts away the unreal, cannot

but believe that the real will survive and triumph—
through and beyond the rough detour and long delay of
man's injustice to man. The skeptic is tempted to discouragement—as are other men. He may be quickly discouraged in his own struggle to assert reality against the
unreal; he may be more quickly discouraged by the magnitude of the task of God in our world where the unreal
is often worshiped as the real. If he clings steadfastly to
the skeptical assignment he will look with clear eyes upon
discouragement itself and see it for what it is—the final
citadel of the unreal. To become discouraged about the
final victory of God is to believe, if only for a moment,
that unreality is stronger than reality. Discouragement is
neither more nor less than denial. God, who sustains human freedom even in its waywardness, is able, over the
centuries, to teach freedom faithfulness. To believe in
God is to expect as a certainty the inevitable achievement
of his purpose—as the human race learns its own meaning
and destiny, to do justly, to love mercy, and to walk
humbly. Not to expect the final achievement is to believe
that reality is insane. God has not started something he
cannot finish.

The average skeptic is more concerned with the immediate than with the meaning of the immediate. To look
at present world culture may well produce in the honest
man a settled conviction that unreality is stronger than
God. Untruth and insanity have the best advertising space;
they marshall the largest armies and navies; they own or
seem to own the instruments of propaganda; they invade
the university and the church. On the short view, one
might reasonably conclude that the cause of God is lost.
Right seems always on the scaffold; wrong seems always on
the throne. The discouraged skeptic, if acquainted with
Christian terminology, discovers that he has adopted the
Christian doctrine of original sin—the view that man is
on detour from his own destiny. If man were totally cor-

rupt, the skeptic, a man, would never perceive his corruption; as long as one man perceives the world's corruption, one link with God remains. The skeptic, along with John Calvin and Karl Marx, may nevertheless conclude that every imagination of the thought of man is only evil continually. From this viewpoint, every man seeks his own, not his neighbor's good. Every nation seeks its own prosperity, not the prosperity of the world. Every religion tends to sacrifice other religions to its own pride and will to power. There is material in the present, as the honest man examines it, to discourage a thousand skeptics.

But the short view is too short to be view. Rome fell because the people preferred bread and circuses to bread and wisdom. The love of truth and sanity was atrophied in Roman hearts. Rome fell; Egypt fell; sixteen civilizations in all, on Toynbee's terms, have fallen. Our Western civilization has no guarantee against failure, no insurance against corruption in the leaders and the led. Unreality may capture the soul of the West, as it captured the soul of Rome. Our Western future may be won with Nineveh and Tyre, with Sodom and Gomorrah. The skeptic can only conclude that departure from reality is death—for civilizations as well as souls. The short view sees the fall of human institutions; the long view sees what happens beyond the fall of empires. History did not end with the fall of Rome. History did not end with the fall of Egypt. If the West falls, history will not end with its fall. Failure has been thus far a great teacher of the human race. We learn to avoid mistakes not only by avoiding them but also by making them. We have thus far learned all that we can be said to know—which is little enough in science as in religion—from our failures as well as our successes. Our freedom operates not outside but inside a context of responsibility, unconditional divine sovereignty. A child can become a man only by learning and growing; the whole human race can and will reach creative maturity only by the same process. The fall of empires has demonstrated that the truth will out, that untruth possesses no permanence. The fall of civilizations demonstrates that unreality destroys its worshipers. God weighs nations and men in the balance and finds them wanting, yet presses forward with other nations and other men toward the goal.

History is like a human life; at the moment we are not farther along than adolescence. A basketball coach once put it this way: "From the time you are thirteen till you are twenty-three, you are practically insane anyhow." The human race is not in its senility but its adolescence—its chaos, its period of exploration, its experiment with all the avenues to futility. Adolescence is unquestionably another word for prematurity. A child cannot become an adult without the pedagogy of adolescence. The human race is now an adolescent, and it does not yet appear what it shall be. Reality may or may not be foolproof, but it has thus far proven many fools. God is the teacher, the pedagogue, the adequate guide. Mankind, like any adolescent, will pass through prematurity to creative maturity —brought by reality to reality—for God is the goal, the goad, and the road.

The human race, in fact, may still be in its childhood, with the full chaos of adolescence yet to come. Childhood is not as gentle, meek, and mild as sometimes assumed. Children, who dislike cruelty to themselves, are often happily cruel to others. The first experiment in civilization, the enterprise of Sumer and Akkad, began only six or seven thousand years ago. No astronomer has predicted less than six million years for our earth to remain inhabitable. And there are other planets. On these figures, the experiment of civilization is in its childhood indeed; it has hardly entered school. The child is still playing with razors and knives; he often wounds himself and destroys valued possessions. He is not yet fully housebroken. The demon in him is not yet fully exorcized. His energy has not yet found its purpose.

One can pass from A to C only through the painful B. Reality is a teaching or creative enterprise; at the present we are not more than half-finished souls in a half-finished world. God, who produces some kind of maturity in every adolescent, who often produces creative maturity in particularly troublesome adolescents, will inevitably produce creative maturity in the human race. The first is not the seed, but the perfect. The important thing is not childhood, nor even painful adolescence, but creative maturity. The goal has existed from the beginning; through man's deviations toward unreality he learns what the real is. Our destiny is older than our journey. To doubt the sufficiency of God is to believe that unreality is final. If unreality is final, the work of the skeptic is finished.

God Compels Growth

God coerces the learning process. To begin with, he evokes questions, even insufficient ones. Man is a questioning animal; God has made him so. Questions are not answers, but in every question the answer is implied. Questions are not luxuries but necessities, not forms of heresy but forms of orthodoxy; they are often both relevant and reverent. God is not outraged when men ask questions; he is outraged when they do not. Human institutions claiming infallibility are quickly outraged by questions; they seek to dope the public mind, to silence criticism, to burn the critic at the stake, to subject the questioner to senatorial inquisition, to make him an outcast to his employer and his friends. God keeps the questions coming, makes them more and more relevant, till infallible institutions display their fallibility in public and men are freed from tyranny. God forced the early Americans to question English "taxation without representation" and "the divine right of kings"; every effort was made to silence the questioners, but reality cannot be silenced. The questions grew, and grew more intelligent, till the American people asserted their right to self-rule—in the presence of their enemies.

The institution of human slavery was unquestioned for centuries. The few who raised questions were quickly outvoted. Yet God compelled the questions; the questions grew, and grew more insistent; they demanded answers. Slavery was abolished—in theory if not as yet altogether in fact.

Nazism grew in Germany because the questions were few or irrelevant. Relevant questions were silenced by midnight raids and torture chambers. The Gestapo was substituted for the gestation of ideas. Propaganda confused the questions, turned the masses against the questioners. Yet men continued to ask questions; the questions grew more relevant and demanded answers. The world was slow to act; the amazing thing is that it acted at all—so slow is human comprehension, so slowly do men penetrate to the real.

The Hindu caste system is strengthened by natural habit and religious sanction; relevant questions are few and timid. Yet God compels the questions; the questions will grow till they crush the infamy, the intolerable tyranny, the crippling burden on the spirit of man.

God not only compels questions, even insufficient ones, but also compels answers, even incomplete ones. The trouble with an incomplete answer is not that it is incomplete but that it is regarded as complete, and thereby frustrates growth. When an incomplete answer is regarded as incomplete, it is a guide to further thought, the basis of experimental action; it avoids the sin of idolatry; it does not impede growth. Science is a set of incomplete answers, yet man's invaluable ally. God compels insufficient questions and incomplete answers among children, then better but still insufficient questions and better but still incomplete answers among adolescents, then still better but still insufficient questions and still better but still incomplete answers among adults—from generation to generation; growth, slow in preparation, sudden in crisis, does take place in history.

A man may say: "I see no hope for growth; men are mentally and morally lazy; they do not want growth." But God thrusts men, with or without their consent, first to easier questions and then to harder ones. Some men resist growth and die; others resist death and grow. Some institutions resist questions and succumb to atrophy; others resist atrophy and welcome questions. As Lincoln knew: you can fool all the people some of the time, and some of the people all the time, but not all the people all the time. God breaks through inadequacy—till growth occurs.

God Has No Permanent Problem World

Our thinking, our interplay of question and answer, occurs not outside but inside reality. Our thinking is conditioned, disfigured, and distorted by premature finality; our growth is frustrated by commitment to the unreal. All the time, whether in growth or resistance to growth, we think within thinking reality. God, who sustains our thinking, resists only our resistance to growth. Our thinking is not alien to God; it is the nature of God. Our thinking is limited by false information, false prejudice, and false objective; reality "thinks" without inaccuracy; God distinguishes the true from the untrue, the abiding from the impermanent. Our thinking, which occurs within divine thinking, cannot be wholly "other."

If thinking is outside reality, it is illusion. To call thinking unreal is to describe not its nature but its premature conclusions. If thinking is alien to reality, it is without father or mother or length of days. Our thinking is neither without parents nor illegitimate; it is a native son, a child in the house, an heir to the throne.

The new occurs; growth takes place—because God's will for us is more than our inertia. The conflict between what we have thus far achieved and what God demands makes thinking possible. Our thinking is not outside but inside God; he has produced us in the first place; it is he who teaches us, compels us, to think; he accepts our right to think and rejects our insufficient conclusions; he teaches us his nature and demand; he stays with us till the lesson is learned; beyond our brief affair with unreality we find, and wed, the real. The unreal, at times, is attractive, seductive, fascinating; but infinite beauty and charm belong only to God. The contest between unreality and God is unequal. We, who are real, have given unreality the only strength it has. Unreality is more *absurd* than *surd;* the only *surd* (an unchangeable factor) is the nature and demand of God. Untruth and insanity in our experience are so many departures from reality. They have power for the moment because they are mixed with reality. They were strong enough to crucify Jesus the Christ, but beyond his crucifixion remains the continuation of his rule in the consciences of men. The medium of the revelation was assassinated; the revelation remains. Untruth and insanity often crucify reality but they cannot conquer it. Beyond every delay of God's will is a new demonstration of its inevitability. God outvotes our rejection and carries us onward toward fulfillment. The human spirit lives and moves and has its being within the care and control of the Holy Spirit. The student is sustained in the school; whole fulfillment is in the curriculum. God is stronger than unreality; his nature and demand will be realized on earth as in heaven. As Isaiah foresaw, "The earth shall be full of the knowledge of the Lord as the waters cover the sea."

If we lived and moved and had our being within an insane world, if the nature and demand of reality were insanity, then insanity, and further insanity, and final total insanity would be our goal. If we lived and moved and had our being within untruth, if the nature and demand of reality were untruth, then untruth, and further untruth, and final total untruth would be our destiny. If we lived and moved and had our being within unreality, if the nature and demand of the universe were unreality, then unreality, and further unreality, and final total unreality would be our *finis;* we would arrive—at oblivion. Because we live and move and have our being within God, whose nature and demand is truth, whole faith and whole skepticism have their task in the present, and whole fulfillment its date in the future. We are predestined to live, to move, to journey, but also to arrive.

Creativity is tougher than we have realized, tougher than uncreativity. As Paul put it: "Where sin abounded, grace did much more abound" (Romans 5:20). The sword conquers for a time; God conquers the sword. Crisis is a stage in process; judgment is a stage in creation. God is sufficient. His is the total energy of the world; his will is the purpose of the energy; he is the unconditional sovereign; his nature is responsibility, love, fellowship; responsibility or mutuality is his gift to man; the gift was made flesh in Jesus and hung upon the cross under the weight of our rejection; the love of God invaded the hearts of the disciples at Pentecost, and now invades the world. The whole of history exists to be completed in his likeness. The Lord's Prayer is our Apostles' Creed, our commitment to creative faithfulness, our faith that unreality has only a teaching function in God's way with freedom, that untruth has no final power over truth, our shattered world no final strength to resist one world of freedom and faithfulness.

Like other men, we often forget our reason for existence —to serve God and enjoy him forever. But God is faithful; he cannot deny his own nature. We are in good hands. At the end of every alternative to his love, our hearts burn within us as we say:

Our Father. . . . Thy kingdom come. Thy will be done
in earth.

The Church Is God's Will for Man

It is clear that self-sufficiency and skepticism cannot long
dwell together in harmony. Either self-sufficiency or skepticism must go. In my own pilgrimage, by no means standard for all skeptics, one realization has grown: I have something to give, but much more to receive. I have nothing
that I have not received; I have nothing that I should not
give. I am a member of the human race—not a self-made
man. Increasingly I experience a deepening sense of need
for human fellowship—particularly a fellowship of growing minds, content with neither dogmatism nor relativism.
Increasingly I receive, in actual daily fellowship with men
who seek the will of God, a deepening awareness of responsibility or love as an absolute demand, an absolute
gift. Fellowship with committed men strengthens my personal dedication to do justice, to love mercy, and to walk
humbly, to let God possess me, cleanse me, teach me, and
make my life a blessing to my neighbor. In actual fellowship with God's Church—where I live—an insistent, irresistible call reaches me: to work together with all men of
good will toward freedom and faithfulness in the total
life of this world. The desire to play the religious aristo-
crat, the ascetic, to withdraw to an isolated island of pride,
of self-sufficiency, grows steadily weaker; the desire to
share the faith and hope and love of men grows steadily
stronger.

Jesus said: "My Father's house shall be called the house
of prayer for all nations." Prayer is growth in the effective
service of God and man. Jesus prayed. His disciples prayed.
Men of all religions pray. I am not good enough not to
pray, not wise enough to withdraw from those who pray.
If my church is less than it ought to be, I share the responsibility to make it a clearer channel of love-in-action

in and for humanity. It is better to light a candle than to curse the darkness. Reality is more than my grasp of it; I can therefore learn from my fellow men, from every man. There is in the present the seed of the future, Christ's Church—a widening fellowship in the love of God. To that fellowship I am called—personally, concretely, daily; in that fellowship I am stronger and better and more than I am alone; from that fellowship a love, a light, and a victory flow from God into the total life of the world; that fellowship is the *revolution* and the *revelation* in our midst, pointing the way to life, leading the way, not without self-giving, to whole fulfillment for all the sons of men.

The Church of Christ is the tree of life, one tree with many branches. Its roots reach backward into the entire spiritual history of mankind; its leaves spread healing into every labor union, every race, every social class, every political creed; its inevitable fruit is the end of all our fragments, the beginning of one world. Our churches bear witness, in deeds as well as words, to the final whole fulfillment. The Church, which is God's will for man, will be reached when all men know "that the whole round earth in every part is bound by gold chains about the feet of God."

ABOUT THE AUTHOR

DAVID WESLEY SOPER, A.B., S.T.B., Ph.D., is professor and chairman of the Department of Religion, Beloit College, Beloit, Wisconsin. Much of the material in this book grows out of his work in 1954–55 as Mansfield College lecturer on Contemporary American Theology in the Oxford University Faculty of Theology; and in 1955 as Trinity term lecturer, Manchester College, Oxford University. His other books include *Men Who Shape Belief* (1955), *Highways to Faith* (1954), *Major Voices in American Theology* (1953), *Room for Improvement* (1951), and *These Found the Way* (1951).